praise for *blinde*

"This is the book that every parent shou[ld read] is not afflicted with both bipolar disor[der and] [ad]diction. It explains a mystery about why a parent is reluctant to make their child accountable for their destructive behavior and instead, chooses to believe their words over their actions. Meg McGuire goes to the root of denial and tells us the story of how she broke the infernal cycle of hope-disappointment-shame-despair-hope."
—Ginette Paris, PhD, author of *Heartbreak, Mourning, Loss: Detach or Die.*

"Meg McGuire's brilliant and moving story, *Blinded by Hope: My Journey Through My Son's Bipolar Illness and Addiction,* returns repeatedly to the tough question of belief: Whose story does one believe? When does hope blind one to the truth? The anguish aroused in struggling to read and act on the true story comprises the dramatic tension that shapes the relationship McGuire creates with her son."
—Dennis Patrick Slattery, author of *Riting Myth, Mythic Writing: Plotting Your Personal Story.*

"Meg McGuire's engaging memoir pulls readers into her fraught journey through the complexities of coping with a family member's dueling diseases. She must confront the dangers of her son's bipolar illness, while also confronting her own denial about his drug use. What should she do for him and for the rest of her family? Ultimately, McGuire realizes she must also save herself. Her growing understanding is an inspiration to us all in whatever challenge we face."
—Kim Bancroft, PhD, author of *The Heyday of Malcolm Margolin: The Damn Good Times of a Fiercely Independent Publisher.*

"This poignantly honest book about one mother's struggle to maintain hope and loving support in face of her son's deteriorating mental health and substance abuse speaks to many mothers treading a similar painful path. In it we may recognize ourselves, our children and the frustrations of engagement with social structures that are often more destructive than helpful and a criminal justice system that is blind and deaf to the reality of these conditions."

—Penelope Joy, Restorative Justice Advocate

"*Blinded by Hope* should be required reading for parents and professionals who deal with children and families coping with addictions and/or mental illness. Meg McGuire's authentic journey between hope and heartbreak clearly illuminates the veil that we as parents wear when we cannot see the truth of our child's illness. A captivating memoir, *Blinded by Hope* stands alone as a guide along the treacherous path of a loved one's substance abuse and mental illness."

—Marti Glenn, PhD, Clinical Director, Quest Healing Retreats blinded by hope

blinded by hope

My Journey

Through My Son's

Bipolar Illness

and

Addiction

MEG McGUIRE

SHE WRITES PRESS

Published 2017
Printed in the United States of America
ISBN: 978-1-63152-125-6 pbk.
ISBN: 978-1-63152-126-3 ebk
Library of Congress Control Number: 2016944596

Cover design by © Julie Metz, Ltd./metzdesign.com
Interior design by Tabitha Lahr

For information, address:
She Writes Press
1563 Solano Ave #546
Berkeley, CA 94707

She Writes Press is a division of SparkPoint Studio, LLC.

author's note

All the events described in this book are true.
However, in order to protect the identity of the author, the author's family members, friends, doctors, and members of the community, the names and identifying characteristics of some characters have been changed. In the cases where real names are used, they are done so with permission.

To my son
for your perseverance and courage
in dealing with your challenges.

To all the family members who are dedicated to getting
effective and compassionate treatment for their loved ones
who suffer with mental illness and substance abuse.

"Until the last moment, anything is possible."

—The Dalai Lama

"There's a comfort in the strength of love;
'Twill make a thing endurable, which else
Would overset the mind or break the heart."

—Wordsworth, from "Michael"

contents

blinded by hope

prologue

The San Francisco Superior Court judge looked at my son, whom I will call Ryan, as he passed sentence on him for receiving a stolen laptop and being present at a burglary. "You come from a good background, you've had a good education, you've suffered no hardship. Four years."

The judge could have sentenced him to two years. It was a first incarceration. I think he got some pleasure out of putting a white, college-educated man in his place. Four years. He also ignored my plea at the sentencing hearing to take into consideration the factor of Ryan's bipolar illness.

It was the words "you've suffered no hardship" that stabbed me to my core. My forty-three-year-old son had been struggling for twenty-two years with the dual curses of bipolar illness and drug addiction. It was—and still is—a hardship for us all: Ryan, his father, his sister, and me.

What did the judge know about the trials of a family coping with a brain disorder? About the hardship of a mother whose heart broke over and over each time her son was hospitalized, each time he was fired from a job, each time a woman he loved said "enough" and left him? For twenty years, each time the phone rang late at night, I was terrified to answer.

The judge didn't know what it's like to be called to the hospital early in the morning and see your son strapped down in four-point restraints, half out of his mind, screaming, "Ma! Ma!" over and over.

The penal system that incarcerates the mentally ill, rather than providing treatment, is an injustice. Even people who care about me express their intolerance and prejudice about those with a mental disability. One close friend said, "Well, now at least you know where he is—in prison, not homeless on some street."

I keep chasing a dream that one day I'll wake up and Ryan will be the bright, promising artist he seemed destined to be before mental illness rewired his brain. The unfairness is that mental illness is stronger than a mother's love.

chapter 1

how did it come to this?

We hadn't planned to get married. Not then, anyway. We were both twenty-one, college seniors. I had just been awarded a full fellowship to attend graduate school at the University of Virginia, and Jerry was planning to attend law school at the University of Pennsylvania. We would see whether our love could withstand the geographical distance. That's when we found out I was pregnant—a result of too much partying on St. Patrick's Day.

We would get married. We didn't even discuss other options. It was 1967, and that's what girls and boys from Irish Catholic families did. My mother flew into a rage. Her attempt to keep me chaste by flipping the front porch light on and off every time Jerry brought me home from a date had failed.

No, she said, she didn't want to see the ring Jerry had given me the night before when we'd broken the news to his parents. Jerry's father had wisely said, "Your mother is not going to be happy about this." He was right. We all knew how volatile my mother could be.

The day before, I had called my father to tell him I was pregnant and made him promise not to tell Mom. Jerry and I wanted to break the news to her ourselves. Dad did not keep his promise. As soon as we came into the house, Mom told Jerry to get out and yelled, "If you think you're going to get married, you'll have to find a priest in another state." She would not allow me to wear white in *her* home parish in New Jersey.

We found a wonderful priest at St. Francis of Assisi Catholic church in Manhattan, where I had often attended noonday Mass in the summer. Father Joseph was kind and compassionate, and we needed his compassion. Since we were not being married in our home parish, he asked us each to sign papers stating there was no "impediment" to the marriage.

"Are you marrying of your own free will?" he asked me.

"Yes, of course I am. What's an impediment?"

"Being underage, having a certain physical defect, marrying your first cousin, or having already been married."

I nodded my head. And then he continued. "Marrying because of being pregnant could also be viewed as an impediment."

"How could pregnancy be an impediment? It's not a physical defect."

"Because you might feel you are being forced to marry," he said, loosening the collar of his cassock.

I wanted to say, *What about Mary? Wasn't she pregnant before she married Joseph?* Instead, I said, "If that's the case, I can't sign the document."

I didn't know whether he suspected that I was pregnant, but I wasn't going to sign a document saying I wasn't.

"It's only a formality," he said. "You should just sign it and get it over with. I'll give you a couple of minutes to think about it."

He excused himself to get Jerry, whom a friar was counseling.

"What's holding things up?" Jerry asked.

"I can't sign this document. It's a lie."

"I know it's a lie, but we want to get married, so just sign it. I want to get out of here."

* * *

A small group of family and friends attended our wedding, and my uncle Joe, a diocesan priest from Long Island, officiated at the Mass. The night before the wedding, I asked my father to meet with Jerry and tell him I couldn't go through with it. I had horrible morning sickness and felt much too rushed. The life I had mapped out for myself had been altered forever. Dad called Jerry and arranged to meet him for breakfast, but Jerry never showed. Or at least that's what my father told me.

When we got to the church, Jerry was waiting for me at the altar, oblivious to my distress. When my uncle asked, "Do you take this man to be your lawfully wedded husband?" I couldn't answer through my tears. My uncle took a breath and paused, waiting for me to compose myself. He then looked me in the eye and repeated, "Do you take this man to be your lawfully wedded husband?" I still couldn't open my mouth, and my face was wet. Uncle Joe leaned in closer to me and whispered, "Meg, you have to pull yourself together and say something." I couldn't. I had nothing to say.

After several moments of silence, Uncle Joe took it upon himself to say, "I do" and thereby sealed the marriage vows.

I never said "I do," but we were married for eleven years.

* * *

We moved to Philadelphia, so Jerry could attend law school, and I found a job. I didn't think much about the sacrifice I was making by giving up my fellowship to grad school. I deferred my dreams indefinitely. It helped that I loved Jerry and was determined to make a good life with him.

Six months later, our son Ryan was born. Liz followed two years after that. At Ryan's birth, I felt a profound love for him. He had a precipitous entry into the world, crowning in the front seat of the car as Jerry raced me to the hospital. The soulful Otis Redding had just died, and "Try a Little Tenderness" was playing on the radio. Earlier that morning, I had called the law school secretary to get Jerry out of his torts exam after my water broke and my contractions started coming fast and hard. Each time I tried to tell her what was happening, I had to hang up because the pain knocked the breath out of me. At the hospital, Jerry carried me to a gurney minutes before I delivered. Our son has been breaching boundaries, slipping through, ever since.

Ryan seemed fearless almost from birth. He was a sunny, energetic, freckle-faced toddler with a Beatles haircut who bounded into each room. He was always in motion, undeniably *there*. When Ryan was two and Liz was six months old, we moved our family from Philadelphia to Los Angeles, where Jerry accepted a position with a prestigious law firm. It wasn't our first choice. We had wanted to stay in the Northeast, where we enjoyed the changing seasons.

Instead, we set up house in a small rental in Venice, not far from the beach. We quickly embraced the climate and the sunshine. I enjoyed planting a garden of string beans, strawberries, and tomatoes and creating a playhouse out of an old moving crate. We explored the vast metropolis of Los Angeles, taking advantage of the beach, biking and hiking trails, and art museums.

One day at the Pasadena Art Museum, Ryan, age three, spied an installation of Claes Oldenburg's giant, multicolored pool balls in a gallery at the end of a long corridor. Before I could stop him, he ran down the hallway, and hurled himself against the installation like a cue ball. He laughed as the two-foot-high red and yellow and blue balls rolled around the gallery. The guards came running to stop him, but Oldenburg, who happened to be in the gallery, smiled his approval of a fearless child's interaction with his art.

A year later, we went with another family for a snow weekend in Big Bear, a few hours outside Los Angeles. After two days of playing in the snow, building a snowman, and having snowball fights, we went sledding. Ryan leaped on a wooden Flexible Flyer, pointed the sled down a steep hill, and headed toward a large pine tree. He whizzed down the hill, delighted with himself, as we ran after him, yelling, "Fall off! Fall off!" He didn't, and we couldn't catch him. The front of the sled hit the base of the tree, and Ryan flew forward. The next sound we heard was the crack of his skull on wood. It is difficult to describe how loud that crack sounded. I was sure his skull had broken.

How could we have let him get on the sled and speed away like that? I felt completely irresponsible. Terrified, we raced him to the local hospital, but the emergency room doctor who examined him there said he didn't have a concussion. "Just keep him awake for the next several hours as you drive home. He'll be fine in the morning." Miraculously, he was.

Although I didn't want my son to endanger himself, I took some satisfaction that he seemed unscathed after his adrenaline-filled mishaps. But years later, as he continued to sustain injuries from other falls and skateboard accidents, I wondered whether his brain had been damaged on that winter day.

In elementary school, everyone wanted to be Ryan's friend. He ran with a group of energetic boys who were mischievous but never got into serious trouble. They acted like a pack of unruly puppies wrestling, skateboarding, and riding their bikes. He was an exceptionally talented artist who made detailed drawings of ancient ships like the *Golden Hind*, Sir Francis Drake's warship that circumnavigated the globe. When he was in second grade, I took him on a trip to San Francisco to see the replica of the *Golden Hind* docked in the bay. He had a great time climbing the rigging, imagining he was the ship's artist, making sketches of the sailors' exploits capturing treasure.

Like many boys, he was fascinated with Superman and Spider-Man and drew endless pictures of their many adventures. He began taking art classes, and his illustrations were regularly used on many of his school's invitations and posters and published in *Cricket* magazine. His art teachers doted on him. I did, too. I was particularly proud and perhaps covetous of his artistic talents. As a young girl, I wanted to pursue art, but my artist father discounted my talent. "Either you have it or you don't," he said. Clearly he thought I didn't have it. I was determined I would never crush my own children's dreams.

One day Jerry came home from work and announced that he had quit his job at the law firm and wanted to establish his own practice. Without discussion, I became the family's sole financial supporter. My teaching salary at a private school was pitiful. I was scared we weren't going to be able to pay our bills. Soon after that, Jerry's father became ill and died from cancer and Jerry withdrew into himself for many months.

We had been good companions throughout his years in law school and loved parenting our two young children, but our marriage was suffering. We were moving apart emotionally. We tried couples' counseling for several months, but it became clear we needed to separate. We divorced two years later, when Ryan was in sixth grade.

It was a stressful period. I was working full-time as a third-grade teacher and taking night classes to become a family therapist. I wanted and needed a career, and I was also interested in figuring out the dynamics of my own dysfunctional family. Jerry was starting his solo law practice; his ability to contribute to child support was minimal. Although he lived close by and saw the children often, Liz, in particular really missed her dad. Ryan rarely expressed his sadness about the divorce, but he became more preoccupied. I was overwhelmed trying to keep everything together. I didn't realize the impact our split had on either child. I was lonely, and I think the children were probably both depressed. My main memory of this time is of falling asleep each night as I read to them on the couch. I don't think we ever finished the entire *Chronicles of Narnia* series.

The first Christmas after the divorce was bittersweet. Ryan, Liz, and I walked down Main Street on a warm day in mid-December and bought our tree from the Boy Scouts. At home, we set up the tree in a corner near the front window of our living room. As I opened the boxes of lights and ornaments Ryan had retrieved from the basement, I started to sweat and get dry mouth. Odd but true: hanging Christmas tree lights caused me great anxiety.

My mother and father were perfectionists in all things aesthetic, including the hanging of Christmas lights. In the 1950s, thick, opaque-colored bulbs burned in repeating sequences of blue, orange, yellow, green, red, and white. Dad replaced burned-out bulbs immediately. The '60s brought clear glass bulbs of the same colors that seemed to need fewer replacements. The '70s ushered in tiny clear glass lights that danced magically as pin-pricks of white starlight. Each bulb knew its place, its string hidden well by tree needles. Dad said, "Don't ever let the cords show; the lights have to look like they're floating in space."

I inherited my family's Christmas tree lights, as well as a compulsive desire to replicate my memories of childhood magic. My anxiety grew because I could never get them just right. Ryan and Liz referred to my obsession as "Christmas tree light psychosis." They decided to cure it. Ryan said, "Mom, let me and Liz do the lights this year."

"Are you sure? You know what that means, don't you?"

"Yeah, I know you want them done just right, and we can do it. We know what you want. You'll see."

Liz added, "Why don't you go upstairs, and we'll call you when we're finished?"

I was hesitant at first but went upstairs and paced. Finally, I lay down on my bed, looked up at the ceiling, and tried to breathe deeply. My children were taking a stand to alleviate another Christmas tree drama. Had they planned this together in private, or was it a spontaneous gesture? I decided no matter how the tree looked I would appear pleased.

Ten minutes later, Liz called me downstairs. It seemed a little too soon for them to have done a careful job, but I took another deep breath and walked down the stairs.

The lit tree had a rakish tilt. It was clear that the lights were a-tangle. The colored lights from the '60s bunched up on the right side of the treetop, and the white twinkle lights from the '70s drooped around the bottom. The opaque glass bulbs from the '50s were spaced more evenly throughout the tree.

"How do you like it, Mom?" said Liz. "I did the bulbs, and Ryan did the rest of the lights."

"Yeah, I tried to give them a new look; I decided they wanted to be a bit freer this year. So I picked up the colored ones and threw them up over the top of the tree, and where they landed, they stayed. Looks pretty cool, doesn't it?"

I started to laugh. It did look cool. The tree looked happy, like a well-licked ice-cream cone that had started to melt. It tickled me completely. My Christmas tree light psychosis was temporarily cured.

* * *

By age ten, Ryan directed his creative energy into skateboarding. He built successively larger ramps in our small backyard from discarded plywood and two-by-fours he found in the alley behind our house. Over the years, he banged up his shins and elbows practicing new tricks. "Come outside, Mom, and see my new moves." I loved watching his new toe tap or hand plant or wheelie, and I teased him about being a cat with nine lives. He sprained an occasional ankle or wrist but always picked himself up and went on. Even though we made several visits to the emergency room, his behavior didn't seem reckless or extreme to me. He was energetic but not careless. I had not grown up with brothers and assumed that his scrapes were part of a normal boyhood. He was my sunny, bright, athletic son.

After teaching all day, I was usually at the stove, cooking dinner, when Ryan came in from skateboarding. While I was stirring a pot of soup or stir-frying vegetables, he would shape the soft flesh on my upper arm like a piece of clay. Using the thumb and forefinger of both of his hands, he made triangles, squares, and circles with my fleshy tissue. It tickled and was a bit of a nuisance, but when he stopped doing it as he moved into adolescence, I missed the physical affection of this ritual.

He was a normal boy who roughhoused and wrestled with his friends throughout grade school, but this type of physical activity came to an abrupt halt in seventh grade. All of his friends shot up in height, leaving him the shortest in his group. He turned his attention to music when his father gave him a drum set for his twelfth birthday. He took drum lessons and beat out more and more complicated rhythms in the egg carton–festooned garage shed behind the house. Soon, he formed a neighborhood band. Between the sounds of drumming and the roar of skateboards, I always knew he was around. Liz and I had to carve out quiet space for ourselves inside the house.

In high school Ryan was still popular, excelled academically except in math, won all the school art awards, and practiced more challenging skateboard moves. By sixteen, he had joined a local semiprofessional skateboard team that won many competitive meets. He even made it into the skateboarders' favorite, *Thrasher* magazine.

Ryan's hyperactivity or bursts of creative energy still didn't worry me. He reminded me of my father, who seemed incapable of sitting still or relaxing. Dad moved quickly through his own creative projects, like paneling the basement or transplanting rhododendrons from one end of the garden to another. He was quirky, a bit hyper, but he was also a very successful advertising executive. I didn't associate creative energy with a mood disorder.

I had been a single mother for five years when I fell in love with a man named Luc. He moved onto our block, we started dating, and, after he took a long dreamed-about midlife sailing trip from Nova Scotia to Los Angeles, we married. I was happily distracted and may have missed early signs of Ryan's bipolar illness. Ryan has since told me that as early as age fifteen his friends said his mood swings, either quiet or angry, were too intense for them. Sometimes they didn't invite him to do things because his moods were unpredictable. This news surprised me. Ryan's friends seemed fine with him when they were at our house, skateboarding or playing music.

Luc spent his workweek nearly four hundred miles away and commuted home to us on weekends. Ryan was busy with his own friends and never spent much time with Luc. Consequently, neither of us noticed any behavior in Ryan that might have alerted us that something was wrong.

Changes became evident in Ryan's junior year of high school. He started having trouble both falling asleep and staying asleep. At times he woke with a sense of paralysis, unable to move his limbs. "Mom, there's something wrong with me," he said. He was scared. I was, too.

By then, I had become a family therapist working on communication problems between parents and adolescents or between couples; women's issues, including sexual abuse; and terminal illnesses like cancer and AIDS. My new skills did not help me with my own son. I knew nothing about sleep disorders or neurological problems. I took Ryan to a psychologist, who gave him a battery of neurological tests. After three sessions, she reported no specific cause for his inability to sleep. She suggested he'd grow out of it. I wanted to believe her.

Despite his chronic insomnia, Ryan continued to excel, taking advanced placement classes in English and history and receiving art awards for his paintings of the homeless men at St. Joseph's soup kitchen. I know now that sleeplessness, or a "decreased need for sleep," is one of the symptoms of bipolar disorder, but only since the mid-nineties have such new standards emerged to identify and treat bipolar disorder in children and adolescents.

The week before Ryan was to take his friend Jen to his junior prom, he broke his femur in half in an all-terrain vehicle (ATV) accident. He was with a group of his friends in Rustic Canyon in Santa Monica, taking turns racing the ATV down Haldeman Road, zooming over speed bumps, jamming on the brakes, and spinning out. They were having a great time—until, on Ryan's last turn, as he headed into the curve, the bike flipped over on him. He later said that he knew his leg was broken the moment he tried to stand up and crumpled back onto the pavement.

In the ER, the X-ray showed a clean break through the femur. The nurses wouldn't give Ryan anything to alleviate his pain until the doctor arrived. Jerry and Luc, who had each arrived separately, could barely look at Ryan grimacing in pain. Both of my husbands were attorneys who had an aversion to any form of physical distress. Luc fainted at the sight of blood, and Jerry fainted when I gave birth to Liz. The men stayed in the hallway outside the open door of the examining room.

The orthopedic surgeon, a beefy guy who raced sailboats, finally arrived. He immediately put Ryan's leg in traction, and I almost passed out, too, when he yanked the pulley. The next morning, the surgeon inserted a metal rod inside Ryan's femur from his hip to his knee. He reassured us that this procedure was regularly performed with great success in Europe. "The break in his bone will fuse within a year. At that point, I'll remove the rod and his leg will be as good as new."

"What if you can't get the rod out?" I asked.

"That's never happened. It's an excellent procedure."

Ryan spent a week in the hospital on a morphine drip, which worried me. If it was such a simple procedure, why did he need so much toxic pain relief? He missed his junior prom and final exams. His teachers told him not to worry—he had already earned all A's. He spent the summer hobbling on crutches, painting and drawing at Otis College of Art and Design, from which he had received a scholarship. His friend Chris, who was also attending Otis, picked him up every morning in his little red sports car.

Ryan's behavior began to change that summer. My sunny boy became a sullen teenager, remote and dark. He retreated to his room to listen to music, sometimes with friends but more often alone.

In the fall of his senior year, his ability to maintain an A average masked something more troubling. I didn't know what was wrong, and he didn't want to talk about it. I tried to use my skills as a therapist to talk with him, but sometimes it was easier for all of us when he chose to stay in his room.

At first I blamed his bleak moods on the metal inside his leg. We joked because he could set off alarms at the airport when he went through security. But the joke turned serious as a much larger alarm went off inside me. Knowing what I know now, I imagine that his dark moods were related to drug use. Venice in the 1980s was the epicenter of skateboarding. I didn't know then that it was also a hub for dangerous, readily available drugs.

The following summer, before he left for college on the East Coast, Ryan had surgery to remove the rod. It was supposed to be a fairly simple procedure, according to the surgeon, but the rod would not come out. The doctor pulled it out a couple of inches but found that the femur and muscle tissue had grown tight around the metal and wouldn't let go. He had to hammer it back in and sew up the incision.

"How could this happen?" I asked the doctor.

"This type of fusion has never happened before. The rod usually comes out quite easily. I checked with my colleagues in Europe, and they said they've never heard of such a fusion before. Don't worry; your son will be perfectly okay with the rod in his leg—as long as he doesn't break it again." His nonchalance unnerved me. His offer not to charge for the operation was a poor consolation.

Ryan left for college with great anticipation. I was anxious. He would be three thousand miles away at Wesleyan University, in Connecticut. What might happen to him next?

* * *

We stayed in regular phone contact, and I was relieved to hear that Ryan was adjusting well to college. I visited him over parents' weekend in the fall and met his first real girlfriend, who looked like his twin. He spent Thanksgiving weekend with my parents, who lived in New Jersey. Everything seemed fine. The rod in his leg didn't slow him down.

When Ryan arrived home for summer vacation, however,

he was a different person. He had lost any remnants of his play-fulness and no longer had any interest in entertaining us with his offbeat humor. Instead, he was brooding, negative, and often angry. His outbursts startled me; they didn't seem to relate to anything that was going on in the family. I didn't know then that spells of abnormally irritable moods are one of the symptoms of bipolar disorder, so I couldn't judge how much of his atti-tude was due to typical adolescent angst and how much was real cause for alarm. Several of my friends consoled me with simi-lar stories about their children the summer after freshman year. Their returning son or daughter also resented being asked to reintegrate into family life. My friends told me to respect Ryan's privacy and give him space.

At the end of August, we all went on a family vacation to the San Juan Islands, off the coast of Washington. Ryan kayaked, biked, played competitive rounds of tennis with Liz, and cheated at family card games, as he had always been prone to do. He didn't engage in conversations. He let us know he wanted to be left alone. Ryan had been thoughtless at times, but he had never before been deliberately uncaring. He couldn't wait to return to college and drum with Mood Swings, the fittingly named band he had joined as a freshman. We later found out that two of his bandmates had undiagnosed bipolar disorder.

* * *

During the fall semester of his sophomore year, Ryan's life began to unravel further. He liked his philosophy courses and loved his time in the art studio, but he was having trouble containing his anger and irritable moods. In October he called to inform me he was on probation for smashing a window at a fraternity house party.

"I don't know what happened. I barely remember. All of a sudden, there were guys punching out windows, and I punched one out, too. I was picked up by the school police and brought up on charges of drunk and disorderly conduct before the disciplinary committee. I'm on probation for the rest of the semester."

"What does that mean, you're on probation for the rest of the semester?"

"It means that if I'm drunk and disorderly again, I'll be expelled."

"This is really serious, Ryan. How did you get so out of control?"

"I don't know what happened. I really don't. But it won't happen again. Don't worry, Mom."

His reassurance didn't alleviate my panic. What was happening to my son? I was petrified. I had come from an alcoholic family and had seen too many explosive episodes involving family members who denied what they had done the next day. I was aware that kids binge-drink in college; I did myself. But was Ryan becoming an alcoholic? I didn't even consider a mood disorder as part of his growing problems.

It didn't occur to me at the time to make Ryan more accountable for his destructive behavior. I realize now that I was establishing a pattern of choosing to believe his words over his actions. My love and concern for him often blinded me to the truth.

* * *

Each phone conversation after that sounded direr.

"Mom, I can't sleep. I just lie there, and I can't stop my mind from racing. I'm so tired I can barely get up in the morning."

By late November, it was clear that Ryan could no longer function. He stopped attending classes and couldn't concentrate enough to finish his final papers. I suggested that he go to the student health center and talk to a counselor. I called the counselor and asked her to contact me after she had seen him. The next day, I had surgery scheduled to have a benign tumor removed from my neck. I was still sore and a bit groggy when she called.

"Your son is very depressed," she said. "I think it would be best if you made arrangements to come and bring him home."

She didn't suggest that he fly home to Los Angeles by himself. She said, "Come and bring him home."

I panicked. "Is he suicidal?" I asked.

"He doesn't sound suicidal, but I think it would be best if you flew here and took him home with you as soon as possible."

When I phoned Ryan to tell him the counselor wanted me to come and get him, he didn't resist. This was totally unlike him. I expected him to say, "Don't worry, Mom. I'll get to the airport myself." He didn't.

I was in a fog from Los Angeles to Connecticut. I called my sister in Maryland during a layover in Chicago and broke down crying on the phone. "I don't know what to do, and I'm afraid of what I'm going to find when I get there." She tried to convince me everything would turn out all right.

* * *

Ryan's appearance was alarming. He had always been lean and wiry, but he looked exceptionally thin and haggard. He introduced me to his new girlfriend, Holly, and his housemates. Holly had made a cake to celebrate Ryan's twentieth birthday, but the atmosphere was not festive. When I asked his friends what had been going on, they avoided answering me. I stayed at the campus guesthouse near the student health center. As I unpacked my bag in the small, cramped room, I wondered how many other parents had been summoned to take their depressed son or daughter home.

The next day, we began to pack up Ryan's things. Afterward, we visited briefly with each of his professors, who agreed to waive final exams because his previous work had been stellar. They told him to go home and get some rest. Then Ryan took me to his art studio. I was completely enthralled with the smells and colors of the drawings and paintings hanging in the halls of the art building. Each student had a studio of his or her own. I was envious of their time and space to create. I hoped Ryan would be able to return to this environment soon.

His studio displayed evidence that he had been working feverishly. There were over four hundred large drawings and paintings of bananas in every shape and color combination imaginable on his walls and easel. There were blue and gray pastels; bold black, sepia, yellow, and white chalk drawings; delicate paintings awash with watercolor and ink. The bananas were expertly rendered, but their sheer number and size seemed bizarre to me. Some of them were over four feet wide. My stomach dropped. This wasn't just the result of some creative spurt; something else was going on. When Ryan had been in high school, he had sometimes repeated motifs, like the wildfires in the hills of Malibu or the Pacific Palisades that we could see from the boardwalk in Venice, or the homeless men at the food pantry, but he had never engaged in obsessive repetition like this.

We drove to a local concrete supplier in town to get a cardboard cylinder-like spout large enough to roll up all of his work. When we returned to the art studio, we stood outside in the gray afternoon cold by the Dumpster as Ryan carefully decided which bananas to ship home. He left the rest in a surreal burial ground for a mania of bananas.

After he was diagnosed, I was certain his prolific output was the result of a manic episode, as one of the symptoms of bipolar disorder is increased obsessive activity, but when we discussed this episode much later, Ryan told me I had completely misinterpreted his output of bananas. "The assignment for the semester was to take one object and keep drawing it and painting it. I chose bananas because they change, get brown, and curl. I didn't feel a compulsion to make banana images; I could always walk away from any art piece at any time. My sadness came out of the experience of being alone. Everything I had identified with—my friends and my band—was gone. They had graduated and moved away. I wasn't manic. I was depressed."

His explanation surprised me. I had assumed, incorrectly, that there was something bizarre about rendering four hundred images of bananas. My perception was clouded by my fear—real or imagined.

At dusk, we met with the head of the art department, an attractive, lanky, small-college-town professor wearing a plaid wool shirt. He had sad eyes and the rough hands of a man who had worked in every medium.

"You should be in art school or out in the world, making

commercial art," he told Ryan. "We don't have much to offer you here. All we have is painting, drawing, and sculpture, and you've already surpassed your teachers."

He turned to me. "Take him home. I'll write any recommendation he needs."

I was grateful for his compassion. I wanted someone, anyone, to tell me everything would be okay. His kindness helped me get through the day, but I couldn't sleep that night. Eventually, I talked myself into believing that if I got Ryan home, we would get help and, as my sister had said, everything would work out.

The next day, we rode through a lightning storm in a small, almost empty prop plane to catch our connecting flight to Los Angeles. Each wave of turbulence shook the plane violently. A subdued and shaken Ryan sweated profusely and gripped the hand rests.

For the first time, it registered with me: my fearless son was fearless no more.

chapter 2

warning signs

Days after we returned home from Connecticut, I took Ryan for an evaluation at UCLA's Neuropsychiatric Institute, one of the top psychiatric hospitals in the nation. He looked small and drawn as he slumped in the plastic chair in the waiting room. His unshaven face was pale, there were deep circles under his hazel eyes, and his dark brown hair looked like it hadn't been combed in weeks.

"I don't want to be here, Mom. Let's get out of here," Ryan said.

"The counselor at Wesleyan told me to get you an evaluation as soon as possible. Let's see what the doctor has to say."

"There's nothing wrong with me; I was just feeling down. I don't belong here."

I was told to wait while Ryan had his intake interview. I knew therapy was confidential, but I wanted to know how the doctor would assess his condition. After ninety minutes, the psychiatrist invited me in to hear his diagnosis.

He addressed Ryan: "I'm giving you a diagnosis of depression for now, but I can't be certain you are suffering solely from depression. You may have a mood disorder. We won't know that for sure for eighteen months to two years. If you have an elevated mood episode during that time, I would change the diagnosis to manic depression or bipolar disorder."

I took a deep breath.

"Bipolar disorder often shows up in late adolescence, first with an episode of depression, followed later by an episode of mania. You are twenty now, and your history indicates you might be bipolar."

Ryan nodded.

"What history?" I asked.

"You'll have to ask your son," he replied. I looked at Ryan for an answer, but he only shrugged.

I never found out what Ryan told the psychiatrist. He stonewalled me each time I asked, and that only increased my distress. Hearing that Ryan might experience an episode of mania within two years made me feel like I was living with a ticking bomb. How could the doctor have diagnosed such a serious mental illness so quickly?

He prescribed Ryan nortriptyline, a medication that was used at that time to treat depression. He cautioned about possible side effects, including weight gain, constipation, and increased sleep. "It should lift your mood within four to six weeks," he told Ryan. "I want to see you again in two weeks." He stood up to indicate the session was over.

At first, I couldn't accept that my son had a mental illness. Even though I had seen his moods change over the previous two years, I was aware that many college students became depressed at exam time. It was part of sophomore year blues, wasn't it? My close friend Margaret told me she had taken a leave from college for just that reason. After taking a semester off, she returned to finish her studies. Her experience gave me hope that Ryan was going through something similar. I wanted to believe that he'd be fine once he got some rest.

Several days later, Ryan's friends who were home from college came to visit and cheer him up. I became concerned when he and his pals decided to go Christmas shopping. He had barely been out of bed, and I knew that in the best circumstances crowds made him anxious, but he left with them and assured me he'd be fine. An hour later, he called from a noisy shopping center in the San Fernando Valley, feeling claustrophobic and scared. The Christmas lights were too stimulating.

"I can't make the lights stop twinkling in my mind, Mom. They're getting faster and faster."

"Come home," I said. His friends brought him home, and he crawled back into bed and pulled the covers over his head.

Many years later, when I suffered a severe concussion, I could not tolerate crowds or bright lights for almost a year. It was only then that I understood the extreme discomfort of such sensory stimulation when the brain has been injured. At the time of Ryan's experience, however, I was afraid he was losing his mind.

* * *

Most of that winter, Ryan remained in his room until noon each day. He came downstairs to grab some food and returned to his bedroom to eat. He seldom shaved, changed his clothes, or combed his hair. He listened to music all night because he couldn't sleep. He rarely ate dinner with Liz and me, and when he did, he was quiet and sullen. Always a voracious reader, he now said he couldn't concentrate. He wrote letters to his friends at college but didn't want to do any art. "I have no ideas," he said when I suggested he draw or paint. I knew he was severely depressed when he never even took his skateboard out of the closet.

He considered therapy a complete waste of time. He took the bus every two weeks to his appointed session, but he told me he had nothing to say to the psychiatrist. He hated his medication. It had not improved his mood, and he was gaining weight, as predicted. His clothes no longer fit, and he felt bloated. He said, "I look like the Michelin Man, Mom." I was glad he still had his sense of humor. Even though he couldn't stand his weight gain, he began to eat sweets compulsively. Both Liz and I baked a new batch of chocolate chip cookies every week. It was the only thing we could do to cheer him up.

As the months dragged on with no respite from his depression, I became increasingly alarmed. Jerry had gone through a period of debilitating depression the year after his father died. I, too, had become depressed after we divorced. I knew what it was like to feel as if life was empty. I feared Ryan was having a similar experience.

During that long winter, we started to get on each other's nerves. I was frustrated that neither Liz nor I could help lighten his mood. Gloom settled over the house. I suggested he go back to school or get a job. I hoped having a regular schedule with responsibilities would motivate him and change his moods. He started to work part-time at our friend's law office.

After several months, he began to talk about his future. He

thought about returning to Wesleyan but then decided not to. His girlfriend, Holly, had been supportive and in constant touch during that difficult winter and now wanted Ryan to move with her to San Francisco. Ryan decided to join her there, get a job, and take preliminary courses in architecture at the University of California, Berkeley.

I liked the sound of his plans. When he became more optimistic, I thought he was on the road to recovery. I knew Ryan hadn't dealt with the core of his depression and that it could still turn into something more serious, but I believed he had turned a corner. I crossed my fingers and hoped for the best.

* * *

Ryan left for San Francisco in May 1988. He shared an apartment with Holly and another friend from college and found a job with a painting contractor working on the famed Victorian Painted Ladies. His specialty was applying decorative gold leaf at the top of the outside molding on the turn-of-the-century, three-story houses. No one else on the crew wanted to hang from the scaffolding at such a height. Ryan enjoyed this combination of artistry and potential physical danger. He was proud of his work and sounded more solid each time we talked. All the more reason the rather formal letter I received from Holly that summer shocked me:

> *Your son is not functioning as a responsible adult; he is physically and emotionally unstable. He is not, at this time, capable of making proper choices because he is under the influence of a drug. He is addicted to heroin.*

25

*On top of that, he is beset by mood swings that he nei-
ther understands nor realizes the extent of. Heroin, as
well as alcohol and any other available substance, has
become his way of coping with his illness.*

I was devastated by her letter and shaken by our subsequent
phone conversation. Reading the word "heroin" made me physically ill. Ryan's behavior over the last couple of years had sometimes been erratic, but I had never suspected illicit drug use. I
had attributed his long silences and grumpiness to his depression. Now I had to consider that drug use might have contributed to the dramatic changes in his personality.

I chose not to confront Ryan on the phone. He was driving
home to Venice that weekend for a visit, and I wanted to see him
before saying anything. When he arrived, I showed him the letter.
He emphatically and angrily denied the contents. "I don't know
what Holly is talking about. How could you even *imagine* in your
wildest dreams I'd do heroin?" He knew he had me with those
words. Of course I couldn't imagine it, and I didn't know how to
deal with his denial—and, it turned out, my own. I needed help.

I called Jerry about the letter and recommended doing a
family intervention. I had no training in or knowledge of what
was involved in a professional intervention but I naively thought
if we showed Ryan united concern about his alleged drug use,
we could persuade him to go into treatment.

Jerry was willing to meet with us but was cautious about the
contents of the letter. He had never met Holly and had no reason to trust her. He didn't believe his son was addicted to drugs.
Instead, he thought Ryan was just immature and it was time for
him to grow up.

Liz was grief stricken when she read the letter. She knew some of the kids at their high school had used heroin, but she had never suspected her brother. As we talked about it, however, the idea of possible drug use began to shed light on some of Ryan's alienating behavior the year before.

We asked Ryan to meet us in Jerry's law office that Friday afternoon for a family meeting. We hadn't had one since Jerry and I had told the children we were separating, nine years earlier.

On the walls of my ex-husband's office, he still had the lithograph of a tree I had given him when he first opened his practice. Photos of our children when they were younger sat on his desk. I recognized the "client" chairs across from his desk as ones we used to have in our living room. They had never been comfortable. Liz and I sat in them, and Jerry sat across from us behind his desk. When Ryan arrived minutes later, he was sweating and seemed on edge. He stood defiantly near the open door, leaning against the doorjamb, his arms folded across his chest.

I started the conversation in a trembling voice.

"Ryan, I'd like to talk about the letter I received from Holly. We are here today because it scares me to death to think you're using heroin. How could you put something so lethal in your body? If you're using—and I assume you are, because why else would Holly write the letter?—you need help right away."

He looked at me and said nothing.

Liz spoke next. "Ryan, I'm really scared about what you're doing to yourself. I want you to stop."

"I'm not doing anything to myself," he told Liz. "And I don't know what Holly's talking about. We had a fight last week, and she told me to get out. So I got out. But the fight had nothing to do with drugs. I've been depressed lately, and she's not used to dealing with someone who's depressed. She never should have written Mom saying I'm using dope. And, Mom," he said, looking at me, "you know me better than that. I can't believe you would take her word. You don't even know her. I've already told you I'm not using drugs. I don't need treatment. There's nothing to treat."

He was visibly upset. I was still shaking.

Jerry, who put extreme value on people telling the truth, was quiet during this interchange. His elbows were on his desk, his fingers clasped under his chin. He believed Ryan. "If he says he's not using, then he's not using. There's nothing more to discuss." He trusted that Ryan would never lie to him. He was angry with me for making the accusation and for insisting on the meeting.

Part of me wanted to believe Ryan, too. I couldn't square the image of my son shooting heroin from a hypodermic needle into his veins. I considered heroin the worst possible drug anyone could use, the most addictive and the most lethal. I associated heroin users with the dregs of society—not my son.

I also thought about the trouble Ryan had gotten himself into at Wesleyan for drunk and disorderly behavior. Holly had known him then and had experienced firsthand the beginning of his depression. She had no reason to make up this damaging story. She had written to me out of genuine concern for Ryan's mental health.

Still, I chose to believe my son.

Prior to our ineffective intervention, I had done no research about treatment facilities in Los Angeles. I assumed, incorrectly, we would find something once Ryan admitted he needed help. This was long before reality-TV shows documented interventions and rehab. I didn't know plans had to be put in place before an intervention. The protocol was to immediately drive the person from the meeting to treatment. I also didn't know that for an intervention to work, the whole family had to agree there was a problem of addiction and demand treatment. When parents are not unified, it's easy to manipulate one against the other—and that is exactly what our son did.

Ryan did not admit his use and blamed Holly for making it up. He stormed out of the office and drove out of town. There was no weekend visit. Liz and I left Jerry's office completely defeated.

* * *

Neither Jerry nor I knew how to deal with a very difficult situation. Our strained relationship added to our inability to see what was going on. Jerry was defensive and I was in a panic about our son's probable drug use. My fear was compounded by the memory of my mother's denial of her drinking problem. Was history repeating itself with my son's drug use and denial? I felt completely alone.

Ryan drove back to San Francisco that night. He moved into an apartment with Gary, a bandmate from college. The distance between us made it easier to pretend he was not using drugs. I tried to keep tabs on him by phone, but our conversations were tense.

Three months later, I got a call from Ryan's friend Jason. "Ryan's in the hospital. It's nothing serious. He just broke his wrist. He's in a cast."

"How did he break his wrist?" I asked.

"He was climbing up the side of his apartment building, trying to break in. He forgot his key."

My heart raced. "What do you mean, he was climbing up the side of the building?"

"He thought if he got to the balcony, he could get into the apartment."

"Was he high on drugs?"

"I can't say."

I booked a flight to San Francisco.

Had this been the manic episode the psychiatrist had warned about, or had Ryan been high on drugs? I needed to see his condition for myself, and I wanted to meet his roommate, Gary. Ryan had told me Gary came from a "family of professionals" in Boston and wrote most of the lyrics for their band. The other members of Ryan's college band were now living in San Francisco, busy recording demos and playing local clubs.

Ryan, his arm in a cast, initially seemed happy to see me but became increasingly jittery. While Ryan, Gary, and another band member talked among themselves, I excused myself to use their bathroom. That's where I saw, in full view under the sink, a hypodermic needle, rubbing alcohol, a spoon, and matches. Even I knew these were the paraphernalia of heroin users. Ryan had lied to me. I felt like a fool for believing he hadn't used. I pulled myself together, but I was at a loss about how to deal this new betrayal.

We left for our scheduled dinner in North Beach. During dinner we made small talk, until I could contain my anger no longer. I blurted out what I had seen under the bathroom sink. Ryan and Gary responded with blank expressions. I asked Gary when he had started using heroin and why. He told me some story about how the famous artists of the 1920s and '30s used opium and heroin to enhance their creativity. As a musician, he believed it heightened his creativity, too.

I directed my rant at Gary. "You might think it's cool to shoot heroin into your veins. You might even believe it's going to make you a better musician. But you're fooling yourself. Maybe you'll be able to experiment and have no negative side effects. Ryan can't take that kind of gamble. For him, experimentation could lead to serious addiction." My heart was beating so hard I had to stop to take a breath. "If you ever inject my son again, I will personally break every bone in your body."

Gary blanched and excused himself to go to the bathroom. Ryan said nothing to defend himself, nor did he deny that I was speaking the truth. He turned away when I told him he was jeopardizing both his health and his relationship with me.

By blaming Gary, I held my son blameless. In my reasoning at the time, Gary must have injected my son with heroin. Ryan wouldn't have put drugs into his own veins. This became our pattern for years. I believed the lies Ryan told me. What I could not bear to believe he was doing to himself, I blamed on others.

Gary packed up his things the next day and moved out. He called from somewhere in the Southwest to say he was returning to Boston. Ryan called me to complain. "Now I'm left with the responsibility of the entire rent, and it's your fault Gary left."

"*My* fault? How about taking responsibility for what you and Gary were doing?" I was thrilled Gary was gone. His absence might not prevent Ryan from getting drugs, but I naively thought there might be less reason for Ryan to use now.

For the next seven months, Ryan worked at his painting job, took art classes, and was accepted as a painting major at the

San Francisco Art Institute. He moved into a more affordable apartment and saved up enough money to take a six-week summer trip to Europe with two high school buddies. During that time, he also saw the inside of three emergency rooms for what I was told were skateboard injuries. I now suspect, however, they may have been for drug overdoses. I didn't yet understand the dynamics of Ryan's illness—the denial, the avoidance, and the easy manipulation of the truth.

chapter 3

the bike ride

At the end of the summer, my husband, Luc, and I rented a house on Cape Cod for a family vacation. The plan was for Ryan to join us when he returned from traveling in Europe. When we met him at the bus depot on the Cape, he looked haggard. It was clear he hadn't slept for days. At dinner he was anxious and rambled on and on about nothing intelligible. He spent a sleepless night on the couch, watching *The Godfather: Part II*. The next morning he said, "The sun's too bright," and refused to join us at the beach. When we returned in the late afternoon, he was still on the couch, eating a bowl of cereal, watching the same movie, and shouting, "Al Pacino is the man!" This disturbing behavior continued for days.

He was too tired to go biking with his sister, Liz. Instead, he gave her a medieval deck of tarot cards he had bought for her in Spain. She shuffled the deck and asked him to pull cards for a spread. We shuddered when he picked the hangman.

On the plane ride home from Boston to Los Angeles, Ryan was extremely agitated and suspicious of other passengers. I tried to soothe him by talking softly, but he kept leaning forward and interrupting other passengers' conversations. "You don't really mean that, do you?" he said to the middle-aged woman sitting across the aisle. At first she looked puzzled, then conferred with her husband and asked the flight attendant to change their seats. Ryan started to sweat profusely. "I need to get some water, Mom." He paced up and down the aisle until the flight attendant told him to sit down and stop bothering others. I was embarrassed. I saw other passengers looking at me like I should be doing something to alleviate the situation but I didn't really know what to do. He took his seat, buckled his seat belt, and said, "You okay, Mom? I hope you're okay. It's really hot in here."

"I'm fine," I said. "You're the one I'm worried about."

"Oh, I'm okay; it's just too hot in here. I can hardly breathe. I need to get out."

"Well, you can't get out, so why don't you listen to your music?"

"Right." He slipped his headphones over his ears, settled back into his seat, and listened to his music, gulping for air. I could barely breathe myself, hoping there wouldn't be an incident. It was a long plane ride home.

* * *

When we arrived home, Luc had to leave for work in Sacramento and Liz left to visit her friends in Santa Barbara. That night Ryan still couldn't sleep. He was afraid to be alone so he didn't want to sleep in his room. He set up a mat on the floor next to my bed and curled up, clutching his old one-eyed teddy bear and a stuffed red dust devil he had won as a child. He stayed awake all night, talking endlessly.

"You have no idea how great heroin is, Mom," he said. "You have to try it sometime. There's nothing like it."

Why was he telling *me*, of all people, about the thrill of heroin use? His comment seemed completely random. I had seen his works in his apartment, but I still didn't think his recent behavior was drug related; I thought it was more like a nervous breakdown. His speech was rapid and urgent, and I couldn't understand what he was rambling on about.

I was scared to be alone with him, and I didn't know what to do. I hoped Ryan would just wear himself out and fall asleep. My plan was to call his former psychiatrist in the morning and take him in when Luc and Liz got home. Around dawn, he was still mumbling when I fell asleep. Later, when I awoke, Ryan was gone.

I called Jerry to see if Ryan was at his house. He wasn't. Several hours later, Jerry called to tell me that Ryan had phoned, asking Jerry to pick him up in Malibu. Ryan had jumped on his bike at dawn and pedaled thirty miles up the Pacific Coast Highway to prevent an earthquake. "An earthquake?" I asked. "What earthquake?"

An hour later, Jerry dropped Ryan off at my house. When I asked Ryan why he rode his bike up the coast, he said, "I was trying to exhaust myself so I could fall asleep. If I don't get some sleep soon, I'm going to lose my mind. I had to get as far away as possible from you and Liz, because if I didn't, I was afraid I'd cause an earthquake. If I stayed home, the San Andreas would slip."

"You can't cause an earthquake," I said gently.

"Oh, yes, I can. An earthquake's coming. I can feel it."

* * *

He didn't let me out of his sight for the rest of the day. When I used the bathroom, he waited outside the door like a young child. We walked down the boardwalk to the local produce market, and along the way, he wanted to give money away to every homeless person we saw.

"Mom, don't you have another dollar? Give him another dollar," he said, as I handed him money to give to an older man.

"No, we need it for groceries."

"Just another dollar, Mom. I can tell he really needs it." I shook my head.

When we got to the market, he sorted through the fruit bins and started biting into the bananas, peaches, and plums. "Don't do that," I said. "We'll have to buy them." I felt as if I were with an out-of-control two-year-old.

Luc and Liz had not come home yet, and I didn't want to try to take Ryan to the psychiatrist by myself. I was afraid he'd jump out of the car. The doctor offered to come into his office early the next morning, a Saturday. Days later, after Ryan was hospitalized, my friend Allison, also a therapist, said, "Why didn't you call me? I would have come to help you. Or why didn't you call the police?"

"I didn't even think of calling the police," I said. "That would have made it too real. And I didn't call you because I didn't want to bother you." The truth was, I didn't want anyone to see Ryan in his condition or admit that I didn't know how to handle the situation.

The next morning, Luc, Liz, and I took Ryan to the psychiatrist and he immediately told us to take him to the ER at UCLA's Neuropsychiatric Institute, where he had first been diagnosed with depression eighteen months earlier.

"Your son is quite paranoid," he said. "Make sure you have a person on either side of him in the car, because he'll probably bolt when he sees you're taking him to the hospital. I'll call ahead and issue a code 5150; then, if he jumps out of the car, the police will be able to pick him up."

I had hoped the psychiatrist would simply give Ryan a sedative to calm him down and help him sleep. I wasn't prepared for his immediate hospitalization.

I drove while Luc and Liz sat next to Ryan in the backseat. When we got to the hospital, they each took one of his arms and escorted him firmly inside the ER, without a struggle. He was immediately put on a gurney and wheeled into an examining room. A young, blond psychiatrist requested that we stay in the examining room while he interviewed Ryan. The doctor asked Ryan what he'd been up to. When Ryan said he'd just visited Amsterdam, the psychiatrist asked if he had taken any street drugs. "Hashish," Ryan said. The doctor smiled sadly, shook his head, and said, "How did you take it: in a brownie, or did you smoke it?"

"In a brownie. There are cafés all over where you can get hash cookies and brownies."

"Well, there's a lot of bad dope in Amsterdam," said the doctor, looking at me. "Sometimes it's laced with strychnine."

Did he just say my son was poisoned?

He told Ryan, "You're going to have to detox before we can evaluate what's going on with you. Let's get some tests going, and then we'll decide about getting you a room."

"What do you mean, a room? I'm fine. I just need to sleep."

"We'll take care of that, too."

Jerry joined us in the examining room and talked nervously with Luc about his recent law case. It irritated me that he was discussing work when his son was in distress. Ryan continued to ramble on as nurses took his blood. After four hours, the psychiatrist found Ryan a bed on the psych ward and admitted him on a seventy-two-hour hold for observation and treatment.

We followed Ryan as he was wheeled upstairs. I recognized the jarring sound of the heavy metal door shutting behind us. As a young psychiatric caseworker in Philadelphia, I had worked on locked wards. It wasn't what I wanted for my son.

Ryan started screaming, "Don't let him in! Don't let him in!" He was referring to his father. "Anyone but him." Why was he so vehemently opposed to Jerry being there? The nurses gently suggested that Jerry leave the floor.

* * *

Ryan spent two weeks on the psych ward. He was treated with various medications, attended daily group therapy sessions, met with his psychiatrist and social worker, made a black leather belt in art therapy, and talked endlessly with his friends by phone. He didn't seem to care that he made his sister uncomfortable when he joked with Tony, a patient with Tourette's syndrome, who had a crush on Liz.

"Hey, Tony, you're going to be my brother-in-law," Ryan yelled when Liz and I came to visit. He took out his anger on me in Ping-Pong games by aiming his bullet serves at my head. I knew he held me responsible for hospitalizing him but even in his agitated state, I hoped he could understand he needed help. Yet, his anger scared me. This was a side of him I didn't know.

I visited Ryan each day in between seeing clients and consulting. One night I left the hospital to facilitate a meeting for preschool parents because a new student, who was HIV positive, had enrolled in the school. The epidemic was in its infancy in the late 1980s, and parents were afraid the little girl could infect their children with her saliva. I tried to reassure them. "Your children will not contract AIDS by being kissed on the cheek." As I listened to the parents' full-blown anxiety, I thought, *Who do I think I am? How can I reassure them their children will be safe from disease when I can't keep my own son safe?*

On the tenth day of Ryan's hospitalization, his psychiatrist, Dr. Grey, called a meeting with Ryan and the family. I liked Dr. Grey. A short woman with tight brown curls, Dr. Grey was smart, direct, and compassionate. I trusted her. She sat across from Jerry, Liz, and me, next to a young male social worker whose name I never heard. Ryan joined us, sitting apart from the family. Dr. Grey addressed us all.

"Ryan tested positive for hashish when he was first admitted, but there were no other illegal substances in his system." I was relieved to hear that, considering his talk about heroin.

"After ten days of observation and testing, my diagnosis for Ryan is bipolar disorder, manic depression." She looked at Jerry and me. "Is there a history of alcoholism on either side of your families? I ask because many undiagnosed bipolar patients self-medicate by using drugs and alcohol, trying to manage their mood swings. There's a good chance that Ryan's illness is, in fact, genetic. Bipolar illness is a genetically transmitted disorder." I turned to Jerry, who was looking down at the floor.

I spoke up. "We both come from Irish Catholic families, and, yes, we both have alcoholism in our families. My mother is an alcoholic, and my uncle, her brother, is in recovery."

"My mother's an alcoholic," Jerry added.

Dr. Grey nodded. "That fits the pattern. Many people of previous generations went undiagnosed and tried to self-medicate their symptoms with alcohol. Fortunately, the disorder is treatable with proper medication. When you hear about someone driving the wrong way on a freeway off-ramp, it's usually someone who's bipolar not taking his meds. Someone with bipolar illness thinks he can do anything. His judgment is impaired. Unfortunately, that can often come at the price of killing some innocent person in an automobile accident. It usually takes an average of three hospitalizations for a newly diagnosed patient to accept that he has an illness. It's not something to be treated lightly. This is a serious mental illness."

I could barely breathe. Dr. Grey didn't mince words. Tears rolled down Liz's face as she glanced at her brother. Ryan had always been her hero. He was one of the most popular kids at school—an artist, a skateboarder, and all the girls loved him. It was cool being Ryan's little sister. Now she was being told he had a mental illness. I thought about what his former psychiatrist had said eighteen months earlier, about the possibility of a manic episode. Ryan's behavior over the last two years—his highs and lows—started to make sense.

Dr. Grey asked us how we felt about the diagnosis. I swallowed hard and looked at Ryan. "I'm grateful there's a diagnosis for Ryan's behavior, because you said it's treatable. . . . Isn't lithium fairly successful in managing the disorder?"

Dr. Grey nodded.

"I really don't know much about bipolar disorder," I said. "I was more concerned about the possibility of drug addiction. My entire life, I've seen members of my family struggle with alcoholism and endure the emotional and physical pain they've inflicted on themselves and their loved ones—including me. The possibility that Ryan might be a drug addict was much scarier to me."

At that time, I knew little about the inextricable relationship between addiction and mental illness. In my therapy practice, I had intentionally avoided treating alcoholics because of my family history. I knew I did not have the tools or temperament to successfully confront a client's denial. Addicts are skillful confabulators, and I knew I could easily be deceived. When I was a teenager, my uncle, a priest, went into inpatient addiction treatment for alcoholism. He had received several DUIs and the superior in his parish ordered him to receive treatment.

The social worker at the treatment center requested that our family attend a family therapy session to support him. I was both relieved by and grateful for the opportunity. His outbursts when drunk had always scared me. The session never happened, however. My mother refused to go. "We don't have alcoholism in our family," she said. That was the end of family support for my uncle's treatment. With that kind of denial in my own family, my unwillingness to look my son's illness squarely in the face makes more sense to me now.

Dr. Grey turned to Jerry. "What about you?"

"I don't believe it," he said, shaking his head and looking at Ryan. "I think he's just an addict."

We were all stunned by his response. "Just addict?" I said. "What are you talking about? Last year you refused to acknowledge Ryan was even using drugs. Now you're accusing him of being an addict?" I felt like I was going to explode.

"Why don't you believe it?" Dr. Grey asked.

"Because if he has a mental illness, I'd have to look at that in myself as well."

I sure didn't expect that response. How could Ryan accept his diagnosis, and learn to manage it, if his father denied its existence?

"You'd rather see Ryan as an addict than as having a treatable mental illness?" I asked.

"I'd rather see him control himself," he replied. "I think he can choose to live his life differently. I don't want him to be on medication for the rest of his life."

"What's wrong with taking medication if it helps stabilize his moods?" I asked.

Dr. Grey had obviously witnessed this type of interaction between parents before and made no comment. She explained that most bipolar patients live successful, functional lives if they take their medication, learn to monitor their mood swings, have their medication adjusted as needed, and abstain from alcohol and illegal drugs.

"But," she continued, looking at Ryan, "many bipolar patients refuse to take their meds, because of denial and the desire to recapture the euphoria of the hypermanic mood state they all love. Unfortunately, those who refuse meds often endure multiple hospitalizations."

He didn't look at her.

"I'm going to prescribe Tegretol for you, Ryan, instead of lithium, because it's an anticonvulsant medication used as a mood stabilizer for bipolar illness. One of its advantages is that it will not cause your hands to shake. One of the side effects of lithium is a slight tremor. Because you're an artist, I want to minimize any movement in your hands."

This time, Ryan nodded but said nothing. Dr. Grey asked Liz if she had any questions. She shook her head no; she was still crying.

"How do you feel about the diagnosis and your family's response, Ryan?"

He had been silent during the meeting, but now he was defiant. "I don't have an illness, and my family had no right to hospitalize me. I just got some bad dope in Amsterdam—that's all."

"Well, then, if that's the only problem," said Dr. Grey, "I'd like you to go into a thirty-day rehab program. My recommendation is that you go into addiction treatment while you stay on the medication I prescribe. Then we'll see how you feel."

It sounded like a good idea. Ryan stood up to leave. "I'm not going into rehab. I want to get out of this place as soon as possible and start school. Classes at the Art Institute begin next week."

Dr. Grey replied, "I can't keep you here against your will. You're an adult, and at this point you're not harmful to yourself or anyone else. But unless you stay on your meds and get serious substance abuse treatment, you'll be back. I guarantee it."

Two days later, unable to accept his diagnosis, Ryan left the hospital AMA—against medical advice—with an unfilled prescription for Tegretol. In San Francisco, he found a room he could afford and started school.

The episode left me grief stricken.

I was filled with guilt that in some way my past behavior contributed to or caused Ryan's illness. Research shows—and Dr. Grey had confirmed—that bipolar illness has a genetic component, but

I wondered whether a car accident Jerry and I had when I was five months pregnant could have caused an injury to Ryan's brain. If he was injured, could that have made him more vulnerable to a brain disorder? Immediately after the accident, we were alarmed when the doctor couldn't detect a fetal heartbeat. And there was the lingering shame of knowing we conceived Ryan on St. Patrick's Day, after a night of drinking. Could these events have left him vulnerable to a brain illness? Or was he emotionally damaged because we divorced when he was nine and he found it difficult to shuttle back and forth between two households? Did I harm him by going back to work full-time when he was in kindergarten? Why didn't I notice earlier that something was wrong with him? Guilt, shame, and remorse were constants that left me feeling isolated and hopeless.

I desperately wanted to believe Ryan would take his prescribed medication and stop using street drugs. My thinking was that if he took the medication to fix the biochemical imbalance in his brain, he would return to "normal." But I must have conveyed something quite different to my son. Years later, when we discussed this period in his life, Ryan said, "It really bothered me that you thought I might never recover and be the way you knew me before: 'normal.' I needed to know that you had hope and confidence that I would find my way back."

Jerry denied Ryan's mental illness, and at the time I refused to believe Ryan had a problem with addiction. Both of our belief systems blinded us, but I at least knew he needed treatment. By now, Ryan was twenty-two, and, as an adult, he could and did refuse treatment. Our only leverage was money.

After our meeting with Dr. Grey, Jerry and I went to the hospital cafeteria to discuss next steps. We agreed not to give Ryan any financial support if he refused to go into rehab. Jerry stuck to the agreement. I did not. Instead, when Ryan returned to San Francisco, I helped pay for the Art Institute. My magical thinking was that if he was doing something he loved and had a regular schedule, he would stabilize. This rationale to support Ryan in doing something constructive, even if he didn't pursue the treatment he needed, continued for decades. He knew he could manipulate me, and that became the pattern in our relationship.

chapter 4

bipolar illness

The diagnosis of a mental illness is devastating for the person suffering from the disorder and for his family. When Ryan was diagnosed, I read everything I could to find out more about this relatively common, life-shattering illness.

It affects close to ten million American adults, or about 2 percent of the population age eighteen and older. Another 2.4 percent of Americans have a "subthreshold" form of the disorder that is less severe but can still cause impairment. Approximately one person in sixty will suffer from the more severe form, and at least that many again will experience milder variations. Men and women are equally likely to have bipolar disorder, in contrast with major depressive illness, which is more than twice as likely to affect women. Unfortunately, only a small percentage of bipolar individuals receive appropriate treatment.

Bipolar disorder often begins in mid-to-late adolescence or early adulthood, although, since the early 1990s, millions of children as young as four have been diagnosed and treated for it. It is the fastest-growing mood disorder diagnosed in children today.

In adults, an episode of bipolar illness occurs seasonally, most often in the spring or autumn, on an annual or biannual basis. A major life stressor may or may not precipitate an episode, although the underlying biochemical problems make people with bipolar disorder more vulnerable to emotional and physical stresses. As a result, upsetting life experiences, substance use, or lack of sleep can trigger an episode. Ryan not only had eaten hashish before he had his first diagnosed manic episode but also had suffered from ongoing sleep deprivation for years. Bipolar disorder may have been the underlying cause of insomnia in his teens, as well as the cause of his later substance abuse.

When I first saw the list of symptoms associated with the disorder, it was clear that when we first hospitalized Ryan, he was in the middle of a manic episode. His speech was rapid and pressured, he was giddy and waxed euphoric about the insights drugs gave him, and he wanted to give away money to everyone he saw. He had not slept for over five days and nights. He worried about causing a major earthquake in Los Angeles and subsequently cycled thirty miles up the coast to protect Liz and me. A person having a manic episode believes he has special powers, such as the ability to prevent a natural disaster.

Some researchers indicate that experiencing a manic episode is similar to having a brain seizure. Once a person has had a manic episode, there's a 90 percent possibility he will have another. This is similar to the "kindling" phenomenon in epileptics, in which multiple seizures may result from the first. Having a manic episode can make it more likely that a particular brain will continue to do so.

The disorder is known to have a high incidence in very creative people. William Blake, Samuel Taylor Coleridge, and Percy Shelley, as well as Vincent van Gogh, Anne Sexton, Sylvia Plath, Virginia Woolf, and Eugene O'Neill, suffered from bipolar illness. More recently, Ted Turner, Peter Gabriel, Axl Rose, Jesse Jackson Jr., Carrie Fisher, Lindsay Lohan, and Britney Spears have been diagnosed with it.

A family history of the disorder appears to exist in 60 to 80 percent of cases. There isn't yet an identified gene for bipolar illness; it's a complex combination of both genes and environmental factors. One hypothesis involves a genetic phenomenon known as "anticipation," in which genes become more concentrated over generations and bring about a stronger form and earlier onset of an illness with each successive generation. A study conducted in 2010 concluded that there is a fourteen-fold increase in the rate of bipolar spectrum disorder in children who have a bipolar biological parent. I began to speculate about who was an undiagnosed manic-depressive in my family.

My father, for one, was a good candidate. He was a very successful advertising executive who didn't seem to need much sleep. I never saw him depressed, and, unlike Ryan, he was not besieged by mood swings, but something was off. He could never rest. He worked twelve to fifteen hours a day, and on weekends at home, he paneled the basement or designed a waterfall in the backyard. His constant activity and ambition rattled my mother, who wanted a more stable, simple life. Dad always had some new, grandiose plan for expansion.

My mother was also a creative individual. She decorated the successive homes my father designed and built, but her moods were often quite dark. She was critical and severely judgmental, had bouts of rage, and was physically abusive to both my sister and me. Irish American, she had a fanatical devotion to the Catholic Church and an abhorrence of any mention of sex. She tempered her moods with alcohol; every afternoon she had her "four o'clock beer," a Miller High Life. My sister and I walked on eggshells around her. We never knew when an explosion might erupt. One night, when my father was late coming home, she took all of the sharp knives out of the cutlery drawer, and starting hurling them at my sister and me. As they clattered on the floor, I picked up my sister, ran down the hall and locked her in her room.

Had my mother sought psychiatric evaluation, she might have been diagnosed with a depressive disorder. "I don't believe in it," she said when I suggested she see someone for her debilitating headaches and irritable moods. Instead, she took her troubles to her parish priest in confession, which was more culturally acceptable to her. My father definitely carried the sun in the family, and my mother carried the burden of the dark. They both came from a generation that did not openly explore mental illness or alcoholism—as my mother exhibited with her reaction to her own brother's drinking habit. When I told them about Ryan's diagnosis, they both said, "He'll get over it."

Although there was no indication that either of my parents suffered from bipolar disorder, there was clear evidence of other forms of mental illness in my family. I found out that two of my father's aunts had committed suicide as young women. When I asked my father what he knew about their deaths, he said that at the time, no one talked about suicide; people believed such details of a person's life were private. And then there was my favorite, same-age cousin, Johnny, who committed suicide in his mid-thirties. Even in my generation, talk about mental illness, especially in men, was guarded.

Bipolar illness consists of both depressive and manic moods. The length, severity, and frequency of mood swings vary from person to person. The average person has four episodes of mania or depression during the first ten years of his illness. The manic phase may include feelings of euphoria and inflated self-esteem, overactivity, accompanied by a lack of need for sleep, and an increased optimism that usually becomes so extreme that the patient's judgment is impaired. A person suffering from mania may purchase a dozen mountain bikes if he believes their price will soon go up. One day in San Francisco, Ryan bought two very expensive mountain bikes he saw on sale and gave one to his friend Don as a gift.

Left untreated, a person with bipolar disorder is subject to unusually intense desires, poor impulse control, and bad social judgment. Sexual desire is enhanced during the manic phase, and some individuals lose their inhibitions about anything sexual, including joking or talking about subjects considered risqué. Their speech becomes rapid and pressured, and they have difficulty keeping up with their racing thoughts. Their sped-up internal state can provoke extreme impatience and irritability. These changes in behavior often lead to chaotic and destructive patterns in personal and professional relationships.

The depressive states of bipolar illness are characterized by a flatness of mood, along with a slowing-down of almost all aspects of thinking, feeling, and behavior. The person's concentration is impaired, and his will to do anything becomes almost nonexistent. He has a lack of interest in daily activities, coupled with an inability to make a decision. He can become despairing, sad, anxious, guilty, or hopeless, certain that he will never be happy again. Sleep becomes elusive, appetite increases or decreases, and in the more serious depressive states, the person may have recurring thoughts of suicide.

Although Ryan never talked about taking his life during his depressions, he did discuss the futility of life. In the early years after his diagnosis, I think many of his actions demonstrated a clear desire to destroy himself. The abuse of narcotics or alcohol, for one, can be interpreted as a slow-motion suicide attempt.

There are different types of bipolar illness, and Ryan was diagnosed with bipolar I disorder, which involves manic episodes that can last for seven days and depressive episodes of at least two weeks. He is a "rapid cycler," with frequent, short periods of mood disturbances. Rapid cyclers have as many as four or more episodes of mania or depression per year, and some people experience more than one episode per week, or even within one day. Rapid cycling seems to be more common in people who have their first episode at a younger age, during mid-to-late adolescence. Ryan took some pride in being a "rapid cycler," for a variety of reasons, not the least of which is that that form of the illness is particularly difficult to treat.

chapter 5

the twenties

The following decade was one of contradictions. Everything seemed to be going well for Ryan on the surface, but there were indications that more trouble was brewing within him. He attended classes for two years at the San Francisco Art Institute and got his bachelor's degree in printmaking. After that, he received a partial scholarship to the master of fine arts program in painting at Mills College in Oakland, California. During that time, he was living with his girlfriend, Denise, who became a welcome addition to our family and often joined us for holidays. Ryan continued to see his psychiatrist, who treated him with Tegretol. All seemed well.

There were times, however, when I visited him when I questioned whether or not he was taking his meds. One particular Easter holiday, when we gathered at a rental house in San Francisco's Noe Valley, Ryan was particularly jumpy. While Liz, her fiancé, Paul, Luc, and I were cooking dinner and painting eggs, Ryan kept leaving and returning to the house with hurried explanations.

"I have to have a cigarette"; "I'm going for a walk around the block"; "I'm going out for a cup of coffee"; "I have to make a phone call." He didn't want to use either of the two phones in the rental.

He was never much help in the kitchen, but he usually loved decorating eggs; it was a family tradition. I had collected the eggs we'd painted over the years since Liz and Ryan were young children; each egg had a story we recounted about where we were when we painted them. "Look, here's the rabbit I painted when we were camping in the Anza-Borrego Desert," said Liz. "Here's the sailboat I painted when we were sailing to Catalina on Luc's boat."

When I asked Ryan about his fidgety behavior, he blamed it on his medication. Then he dismissed my suggestion that he call his psychiatrist and check the dosage. The way he was acting, although not as extreme as his first manic episode, reminded me of his restlessness before his first hospitalization. I didn't want to magnify his agitation by watching him too closely—I was afraid my concern would make him more anxious and trigger something more serious—but he knew I was aware of his erratic behavior, and he made it clear that he resented my questions.

In retrospect, I wish I had questioned him more about his medication. But even if I had, it doesn't mean he would have told me the truth or taken my advice. As Ann Patchett wrote about her friend Lucy Grealy, a heroin addict, in *Truth and Beauty*, "I always believed her, if for no other reason than I didn't know how not to." This became a chronic cycle between us: my son, now twenty-four, would not admit there was a problem, and I wanted to believe him. The weekend ended without an explosive episode, but it was clear that Ryan was on edge.

Beyond that tense Easter weekend, Ryan seemed engaged in the rigors of his graduate program and enjoyed teaching a painting seminar to undergraduate students. He spent months preparing for his thesis show, creating six-by-seven-foot canvases depicting bodybuilders' stages of physical transformation.

Even as a young boy, Ryan was intrigued by the musclemen who worked out near our home in Venice. Gold's Gym, the Mecca for bodybuilders in the early '70s, was located at the end of our block. The men swaggered down our walkway on their way to the gym, stepping over the kids at play. Ryan's paintings reflected their grandeur but also provoked questions about the meaning of physical and mythical transformation by showing hybrids of men and animals.

When I arrived at the gallery at Mills, he was even more agitated than he had been when I saw him at Easter. He hadn't slept for weeks while he got ready for the show. He looked thinner than ever, his handsome face gaunt, deep circles under his eyes. He wore pink sunglasses, a floppy tan fishing hat, a short-sleeved garish-print shirt, dark pants, and sneakers. It's not unusual for an artist to make a statement with his clothing, but Ryan's outfit was outlandish compared with his usual dress of understated shades of black.

He greeted friends with nonstop jabber, peppering his conversation with loud jokes and laughter. During the show, his movements were frenetic and he frequently left the gallery to smoke outside, joined by an attractive young woman he introduced as Suzanne, a former painting student. The entire night, Ryan paid little attention to his actual girlfriend, Denise.

I enjoyed the scope and scale of his paintings and the carnival atmosphere of the show, but I was alarmed by his artist's statement. The written description of Ryan's work posted with his paintings was incomprehensible. He was immersed in critical theory, but his statement was filled with codes and numbers that read like gibberish. Several people at the show asked me to explain what it meant, but I could offer no insight.

I flew home that night, both proud of my son's artistic accomplishment and feeling a significant amount of dread. On the flight, my friend Celeste, who had also attended the show, tried to reassure me that Ryan was exhibiting nothing more than exuberance at having finished and presented his work in an exhibition that was the culmination of years of study and expression. But to me, his bizarre appearance, agitated behavior, and incoherent statement signaled that something was desperately wrong. The whole evening seemed like the beginning of another manic episode.

Sure enough, soon afterward, Ryan fell into a depression that lasted several months. He revealed that he had carried on an affair with Suzanne during his last quarter of graduate school. His attempts to repair his relationship with Denise didn't work, and they separated. Ryan's depression was similar to the one he'd had four years earlier at Wesleyan. He felt incredibly sad and guilty about hurting Denise and talked about not wanting to continue to live. He could barely get out of bed that long summer; the only work he could do was washing lithography stones during his part-time job at a print shop.

During this period, I talked to him almost daily from New Mexico, where I was teaching. I was worried Ryan could become suicidal, but I knew he was under the care of a psychiatrist. He was still very secretive about whether he was taking his medication. Once again, because he was an adult and I had no access to his medical information, I was in the dark about what was going on or what more I could do to help him. The only thing I could do was tell his psychiatrist about my concern and offer Ryan a compassionate ear.

Finally, in the fall, Ryan stabilized enough to get a job at a landscape design firm. At first he did simple physical labor, which seemed to suit him. It was important for him to be outside; he liked the physical contact with the plants and trees he delivered to the work sites around the city. In time, he got involved with the actual design and color treatment of the physical spaces the firm was building. He took pleasure in learning about color and design using plants, instead of paint.

Over the next two years, he had a difficult and at times volatile relationship with the owner of the company. During this time, she terminated and rehired him at least twice because of his "attitude and behavioral problems." He blamed his ultimate dismissal on her Irish temper, but he later admitted it was his anger that provoked hers. I wasn't sure what to believe. Was my son unemployable because he couldn't get along with a female supervisor, or did their personalities simply clash?

He eventually found a job as a production artist in graphic design for an Internet networking company. This was the early '90s, when the technology industry in San Francisco was booming and graphic designers were in high demand. The pace of the work was fast and frantic, and Ryan began to react to the stress of the environment with what he himself described as manic behavior. He was fired after two years for personality conflicts with his direct supervisor, this time a man.

I still didn't know the extent of the effect bipolar illness had on people's behavior. When Ryan was stable and productive for a period of time, it was easy to forget that he was bipolar and might still be wrestling with the complexities of the disorder. I was under the illusion that everything would work out. He always seemed to bounce back and move on to the next thing with enthusiasm, which lulled me into a state of complacency. I was constantly surprised and frustrated when events in his life started to deteriorate.

Ryan recognized that time-pressured jobs caused him anxiety. During his time at the Internet company, he was prescribed Klonopin, a medication to help him cope with his anxiety. But when he revealed he was often tardy or missed work, I wondered whether he was using street drugs. His speech on the phone was often slurred, but he attributed that to Klonopin. Again, I didn't know what to believe.

He didn't want me to think he was using, and I didn't want to think he was using. Instead, I focused my attention on providing him with emotional and financial support for his bipolar disorder. I helped him find a psychiatrist and paid for his treatment and medication. In the past, I had strongly suggested rehab for his possible drug addiction, but because he continued to deny using and refused treatment, I chose to maintain a relationship with him, rather than continuing to hound him about his probable use of illegal drugs. Our avoidance of the truth was damaging for both of us.

* * *

Ryan pursued teaching positions in San Francisco, but when none opened up immediately, he took his close friend Don's advice and applied for and was offered a temporary teaching job in the photography department at Lehman College in the Bronx. There was added incentive: some of Ryan's other friends, and Don, who had been one of his best friends since grade school, would be moving to New York, too.

I tried to have a conversation with Ryan about the differences I had experienced between teaching a small seminar at a private women's college and teaching before a very large and diverse group, but he didn't want to hear it. "I know what I'm doing; I'll be fine." I didn't know whether his inflated sense of self and lack of caution were symptoms of bipolar disorder or defensiveness over not having been able to keep a job in the past. My feelings about his move were mixed. I was excited for him to be relocating to the city I had grown up in and loved, and I knew if he was going to pursue an art career, he could have better opportunities in New York. I was concerned about not being close by if his periodic episodes of erratic behavior erupted, but I was somewhat comforted by the fact that my parents still lived in nearby New Jersey, were aware of Ryan's bipolar disorder, and could be counted on if anything went wrong.

In the summer of 1996, he and Suzanne, whom he had started seeing again after his relationship with Denise ended, packed up his van and headed east. During his seven years in San Francisco, Ryan played drums in several bands, one of which was just starting a tour of the United States. They had an engagement outside Chicago during the time he and Suzanne were driving through the Midwest, so Ryan played the shows in Illinois.

Whether because of fatigue, alcohol, or drugs, he was stopped by the police on the highway there for "slow, reckless driving." He claimed that the only drug he had in his system was Klonopin, but he was arrested for driving under the influence.

He was jailed overnight, and a trial date was set for several weeks later. After his release from jail, he and Suzanne continued driving to New York, where they rented an apartment in Brooklyn. Ryan had to hire an attorney to represent him in Chicago, and he returned for his hearing. He was fined but served no more jail time.

Part of me wanted to believe it was reasonable that fatigue, lack of sleep, and Klonopin in his system could make Ryan seem intoxicated. But the fact that he failed the sobriety test meant he must have been abusing alcohol or drugs or both. Still, he was starting a new life in New York and I considered the Chicago incident an anomaly. I calmed my rising panic by continuing to hope for the best.

Ryan taught courses in photography and graphic design at Lehman College during the fall quarter and applied for a full-time, tenure-track position. His studio labs were only twenty-five students each, but the lecture classes were much larger. He found the subway commute and the workload stressful. Although he was told he was one of two finalists for the new position, he was disappointed but not completely surprised when the school passed him over for a more experienced professor. I didn't see him during that first year, but all his phone updates suggested that he and Suzanne loved living in Brooklyn and were busy socializing on weekends with friends in the area.

That year of relative calm concluded when I learned Ryan had been hospitalized at the end of the school year for a Klonopin overdose. I found out later that Klonopin has some of the same sedative properties as heroin and can be just as addictive. The hospital doctors wouldn't give me the specifics of Ryan's overdose, and Suzanne wasn't clear about what had happened, either. Ryan was released after three days and stabilized on lithium. He finally admitted he abused his prescription medication to deal with his increased anxiety about commuting to and teaching at Lehman.

I didn't know what to do. I called colleagues who had New York friends in the addiction field who were willing to see him if he wanted to manage his substance abuse, but he denied he was addicted. When Ryan moved to the East Coast, I looked forward to focusing more on my own life, but having him so far away and not knowing what was really going on made me more anxious. There was no way I could protect him from himself. In retrospect, as long as Ryan denied abusing drugs and didn't want treatment, there was little I could do.

A few months later, Ryan started working full-time in the art department of my father's pharmaceutical advertising agency in Manhattan. It seemed like a good fit. My father had retired, but the art department was happy to give his grandson a job. Ryan had always admired the agency's award-winning work, and he wanted to collaborate with the artists creating the ads.

He assisted the senior art director in designing campaigns, executing computer graphics, and doing production work. He sounded fully involved with and excited not only about the design work but also about researching the properties of the medications the company was advertising. There's some irony in the fact that my son, who mostly denied abusing drugs, was now doing research on drug properties.

When I visited Suzanne and Ryan in the winter, I was pleased to see how calm, content, and relaxed they were. Their cozy apartment was filled with furniture Suzanne's mother had lent them. Photographs and paintings by Ryan and their friends hung on the walls. Suzanne enjoyed creating a warm, homey environment and they both liked preparing meals together. Over the years, Ryan and I had developed a habit of going to art shows together so we visited the galleries that were just opening in Chelsea. It was a joyful visit, free of my usual worries about what distressing thing might happen next.

Before their move to Brooklyn, I had asked Suzanne, who was seven years younger than Ryan, if she was aware of the extent of Ryan's mood swings and past drug abuse. She seemed a bit offended by my question and said she wasn't afraid of his mental illness. She had read about bipolar disorder and believed she could handle the situation because he was in treatment and taking his medication. She also said, "He promised me he would never use drugs again." My antennae went up. Her belief in his guarantee worried me. She was clearly enamored of the image of the man who had been her painting instructor in college, not in touch with the reality of someone with a brain disorder. I doubted he could keep his promise. I was afraid of what would happen when he let her down. His assurance began to fracture with the Klonopin overdose.

chapter 6

new year's day 1998

Big changes were happening in my life, too. I separated from Luc. A long-distance commuter marriage for eight years had eroded our relationship and had been too stressful to sustain. My constant worry about Ryan had not helped. Liz had married and was living with her husband in San Francisco, where she was attending culinary school. I had continued my therapy practice in Venice, written two books on women's psychology, and applied for a teaching job in a counseling psychology program at a graduate school in Santa Barbara.

Ryan visited for the Christmas holidays. It was a delight to have him home again. When he wasn't in crisis, he was always an entertaining companion regaling me with some funny story about what he observed out in the world. He went out on New Year's Eve with some of his old high school friends and came home early New Year's Day.

On that beautiful, sunny day, we stood outside on the front

porch and he told me he had met the actress Courteney Cox, from the popular television show *Friends*, at one of the parties the night before. "She's smaller than she looks on-screen," he said. "Skinny but pretty. She didn't pay any attention to me." He gave me a rueful smile. I noticed his skin looked very pale. Just then, my next-door neighbor, Lewin, climbed the front steps to greet Ryan warmly.

"Ryan was just telling me he met Courteney Cox at a party last night," I said.

"Cool," Lewin said. "What's she like?"

Ryan looked at me, mystified. "No, I didn't," he said.

"You just said you did."

"No, I didn't."

His denial scared me. Ryan put his sunglasses on and abruptly walked through the open front door into the living room. I looked at Lewin and shrugged. Now what? We followed Ryan inside. He stood near the Christmas tree, turned around to face us, dropped like a lead weight to the floor, and started convulsing.

I grabbed a pillow from the couch, got on my hands and knees, and put the pillow under his head so that he wouldn't knock himself out. His arms and legs were flailing wildly. I was certain the Christmas tree would topple over him from all the vibrations. I couldn't find anything within arm's reach to prevent him from biting his tongue. I yelled to Lewin to call 911 and kept trying to prevent Ryan from banging his head on the hardwood floor.

I spoke gently to him, as if I were trying to calm a baby—*my* baby—in distress. I had never seen a grand mal seizure before, but I was sure this was it. Somewhere deep inside me, I thought if I kept holding him and talking to him softly, he could ride this out.

Lewin yelled that the ambulance was on its way. Ryan's convulsions slowed down for a couple of seconds, and then, just as quickly as they had abated, they sped up again. All I could think was, *Oh, dear God, don't let him die.* Blood and saliva were coming out of his mouth and running down his chin and neck.

When we heard the ambulance's siren, Lewin ran out the front door to show the emergency medical team to the house. Ryan was barely breathing. The EMTs rushed into the house and immediately slapped an oxygen mask on his face. They moved me out of the way, lifted him onto a stretcher, and wrapped him in a blanket. A large paramedic leaned over Ryan as he started to come around several minutes later.

"How are you doing, buddy?" he said.

"I'm fine. What's happening?" Ryan said.

"You tell me."

"I was just looking at my mom and smiling," he said weakly, as he looked up at me.

"That's nice, that's real nice, smiling at your mama. You just lie there now, relax and breathe."

A short, blonde paramedic, who seemed to be in charge of the EMT team, asked me to go outside to the porch with her. I didn't want to leave Ryan, but she assured me he was in good hands.

"Is he on medication?" she asked.

"Yes, he's on lithium for bipolar disorder."

"Has he ever had a seizure before?"

"No, not that I know about. He doesn't live with me, but he's never mentioned it."

"Does he use street drugs?" She looked at me directly. No one had ever asked me that before. Certainly no one in authority.

I heard myself say, "I'm afraid so."

She nodded. "Does he drink?"

"He was drinking last night."

"Okay, if he doesn't have a convulsive disorder, he probably had the seizure from dehydration."

I nodded as if I knew what she was talking about, but it was all new to me.

"People on lithium are not supposed to drink. Alcohol dries them out. He's lucky you were with him. Several years ago, my husband did drugs, had a seizure, and died, just like that." She snapped her fingers.

Her comment took my breath away. I felt all the blood drain out of my face, and I got dizzy.

"How old was he?" I gasped.

"He was in his mid-thirties," she answered. "How old's your son?

"He just turned thirty last month," I said.

She shook her head. "They all think they're going to live forever."

She turned abruptly and went back inside to the living room to check on Ryan's progress. I followed close behind.

"We have to take him to the hospital," she announced as she examined him. "He needs to have a complete workup. Do you want to go to UCLA Medical Center in Santa Monica or the Marina hospital?"

"I'm not going to any damn hospital," Ryan slurred.

She looked down at him, still lying on the stretcher on the floor, the needles from the Christmas tree all around him.

"You don't have a choice, young man. And you'd better stop drinking and using drugs. You were lucky your mom was here this time. Next time you might not have someone close by to call for help." He was silent.

"Santa Monica," I said.

She nodded to her fellow EMTs. They put the oxygen mask back over Ryan's face, lifted the stretcher, and carried my son out to the ambulance. A crowd had gathered. As the EMTs carried him away, the woman gave me a form to sign and told me to follow in my car.

I trembled uncontrollably when they left, then suddenly was freezing. Lewin got me a sweater, led me out the back door to his car, and drove me to the hospital. I broke down sobbing in the car. "When is he ever going to learn?"

I spent New Year's Day in the hospital while the emergency room team ran tests. I called Jerry, who lived nearby, to tell him what had happened. He was in the middle of his young son's first-birthday celebration, but he came to the hospital right away. We sat in the waiting room for hours. The doctor in charge wanted to keep Ryan overnight for observation, but he refused to stay. Neither Jerry nor I could convince him to follow the doctor's advice. He had a late-afternoon flight scheduled to return to New York the next day. He wanted to go back to my house and rest.

The doctor put him on Depakote, an anticonvulsant medication, gave him a lecture about abstaining from alcohol while taking lithium, and told me to get Ryan to a neurologist the next day.

First thing the following morning, Jerry and I took Ryan to a neurologist who had treated me for a concussion months before. After giving Ryan the standard neurological tests—evaluating his reflexes, eyes, and ability to count backward—the neurologist said he wanted Ryan to have a CAT scan to see whether anything more serious than partying could have caused the seizure. Again, Ryan refused. I felt as if we were dealing with a rebellious teenager who didn't care about his health or inconveniencing anyone else. Jerry and I tried to reason with him, but he was adamant about returning to New York on his scheduled flight that afternoon.

"I'll get the CAT scan in Manhattan," he said.

We knew he wouldn't. At lunch we talked to him about how he was flirting with death by mixing alcohol with his medication. We strongly suggested he go into substance abuse treatment. He was defensive, arrogant, and angry with us, still denying he had abused alcohol or drugs. We couldn't penetrate his resistance. He wanted to get as far away from us as possible. At that point, I was happy to see him go.

* * *

Two months later, on a Sunday morning in March, I received a disturbing voice mail from Ryan. I had gone out for an early-morning beach walk with my neighbor Amber, the first one we had been able to take in days because of the relentless rain from El Niño's winter storms. The tide was out, and the sea had coughed up miles of driftwood and Styrofoam. We walked along the shoreline, admiring the shapes of the wave-battered wood. Amber picked up a weathered whorl that fit snugly into her palm.

On the way back, we detoured through the farmers' market on Main Street, filled with customers elated that the vendors had survived the winter storms with their arugula, winter squash, ripe tomatoes, and long-stemmed tulips intact. Everywhere, trees were beginning to bloom and the fragrance of freesia heralded spring. I felt lighthearted for the first time in months.

I walked into the house, saw the blinking light on my answering machine, and listened to Ryan's voice.

"Mom, it's Ryan. I got mugged last night, pushed down on the subway tracks; my ribs are bruised, and I have a concussion. I'm ready to make some major changes in my life. Call me."

I took a deep breath, the colors of spring rapidly fading as I listened again to the garbled tones of my son subjecting me to another emergency, three thousand miles away. After his arrogant reaction to the severity of his seizure two months before, I was still angry and wanted him and his roller coaster of crises to go away.

But I clung to his new words: "I'm ready to make some major changes in my life."

I had wanted to hear those words, had prayed to hear those words, but this was the first time I had heard him say anything about making changes. What kinds of changes was he was willing to make? How bad were his injuries? I was cautious. Had he really gotten pushed off the subway platform? When I was working in Manhattan as a teenager, my biggest fear was always that someone would push me, inadvertently or purposely, off the subway platform. My heart began to race. Was this really a mugging, or could he have been involved in a drug deal gone bad? I knew it was pointless to ask him that question. I took a deep breath and made the call.

Ryan answered. A good sign. He usually didn't take my calls; typically, he let his answering machine pick up.

"How are you?" I asked. Did I really want to know? Yes, I did, but I didn't wait for a reply. "What kinds of changes are you ready to make?"

I knew I sounded cold and uncaring, but I didn't know how serious he was about changing his life and I didn't want to get my hopes up. I had been too hurt by previous crises and denials.

For the next five minutes, he rambled on. "The mugger followed me to the subway from a restaurant where I was having a cup of coffee after working late. He had come into the restaurant and asked everyone for spare change. I didn't have any change, only my subway tokens. I opened my wallet. I had two twenty-dollar bills and a single in there, and I gave him the single. He left. I left shortly thereafter. He must have seen the twenties in my wallet, because when I got down onto the subway platform, he came up fast behind me. I should have looked over my shoulder."

"Did he jump you there on the subway platform?"

"I was standing at the edge of the platform with my bag and portfolio. He grabbed my bag and pushed me over the edge. I went down onto the rails. I wasn't going to let him have my portfolio and wallet. When I tried to pull myself up onto the platform, he stepped on my hands and pushed me down again. I tried to get up again, but both times I fell on my ribs. The second time, I cracked my head."

"Didn't anyone do anything to help you?"

"There were only two other people on the platform, and they didn't get involved. I've never been so scared in my life, Mom. I could feel the vibration of the train coming on the rails. A man pulled me up out of the pit when I yelled that the train was coming. By that time, the mugger had taken off with my bag. When the guy got me up, he told me he was a lawyer and handed me his card. I was in so much pain, I couldn't move."

"Did someone take you to the hospital?" I asked, trying to

block out the image of my son writhing on the track as a subway train barreled toward him.

"Three different NYPD squads arrived. They said they knew the mugger; they had gotten complaints about him before. They got me an ambulance to the hospital. I'm going to prosecute that guy when they find him." I shook my head. There was always some guy he wanted to prosecute.

Ryan described his visit to the emergency room. "The ER team did a CAT scan, which showed some blood on my brain. They held me overnight for observation, then released me the next day with pain medication for my ribs."

I said nothing for a minute, but I thought something else had to be going on for him to have such an encounter with a mugger. At that point in his story, wondering if drugs had been involved, I repeated my question. "How much of a change are you willing to make?"

He was silent. I waited.

"I have to change everything," he said haltingly. "My life isn't working."

"What does that mean?" I said, feeling like a piece of wave-battered wood myself.

"I'm ready to go into drug treatment. But," he said immediately, "not to someplace cold."

I had waited a long time to hear those words. For years, I had listened to his words of denial, bravado, arrogance, and contempt. "Readiness" was a sound I had never heard—even if he had added the condition of treatment in a warm climate.

"If you're serious," I said, "I'll do some research."

"I am."

"Good. I'll see what I can find out."

A week later, Ryan flew to Minnesota to enter Hazelden's drug and alcohol treatment program there. Hazelden had one of the best dual-diagnosis treatment programs at the time and had a bed available immediately.

It was bitterly cold in Minnesota.

chapter 7

the early thirties

While Ryan was at Hazelden, I was flying back
and forth from Los Angeles to Florida, where my parents had
moved, and my mother was in the late stages of Alzheimer's disease. I was at her bedside when she died that May, 1998. In July
I closed down my therapy practice in Venice and moved out of
the home and community I had loved for over twenty years. I
made this change to accept a job teaching graduate school in
Santa Barbara. It was an extremely intense time for me, and I
had little emotional energy left over for Ryan's crises.

My only contact with him was by phone. He didn't want
Jerry or me to fly to Minnesota for Hazelden's family weekend.
Because he was in a dual-diagnosis program, which treated both
addiction and mental illness, I was hopeful he would gain skills
to deal with the psychological issues underlying his substance
abuse. I knew that twenty-eight days was a short time in which
to reverse years of drug use, but each time I talked with him,

he sounded more determined to stay clean and sober after his release. "This is really hard, Mom. I just feel awful about myself. I can't believe I've messed up so badly."

His counselor at Hazelden recommended he move into a halfway house or sober-living facility after he finished the program. She did not want him to reenter his home environment because of the temptation to fall into old habits it would present. He rejected the idea; instead, he said, he could maintain his sobriety by going to regular Narcotics Anonymous (NA) and Alcoholics Anonymous (AA) meetings in New York. I was disappointed but remained hopeful that somehow his treatment at Hazelden would help him grow up and take more responsibility for his life and health and the ways in which his actions affected other people.

Other than paying for his treatment, Jerry and I had no leverage and little influence over our thirty-year-old son. I was trying to adjust to a new community and to my demanding and challenging new job. I could only hope that Ryan's attendance at regular AA meetings, visits with his psychiatrist, and medication regimen would sustain his abstinence.

Ryan stayed sober for the next two years as far as I knew, but his substance abuse before Hazelden had already exacted a price. Although my father never said anything, I later learned that Ryan had lost his position at my father's ad agency because of his drug use. He and Suzanne split up, not surprisingly, because he had broken his promise to her that he would never use drugs.

Several months later, after treatment, he found work as a production artist in a variety of short-term positions in different ad agencies in Manhattan and moved to an apartment in the Greenpoint area of Brooklyn, a Polish-Irish neighborhood where my father had lived as a child. He started painting again and dating Diana, who was also a painter, and he picked up drumming gigs in various bands. Although he was having difficulty finding a full-time job, his life sounded relatively stable.

Then, in January 2000, he called to tell me he had just been in the hospital for a third-degree burn on his foot.

I was immediately suspicious. "How did you burn your foot?"

"I burned it in the shower," he said offhandedly. "You've lived in these old apartments in the East, Mom. You know how ancient the plumbing is. The hot water started to come out in bursts and scalded my foot."

"Couldn't you regulate the temperature of the water? Couldn't you get out of the way?"

"No. I turned on the hot water, and before I knew it, it was boiling. The landlord said he would have it fixed."

"How bad is the burn?"

"It's pretty bad. My whole foot is bandaged. It hurts like hell."

I was dubious about what had actually caused the burn or what state of mind he had been in when he burned himself. I imagined he had been high when he took the shower.

"How are you taking care of your foot?"

"I have to go back to the hospital to have the dressing changed. I'm taking extra-strength Tylenol for the pain."

The truth arrived days later, when Diana told me Ryan had been high on heroin when he was admitted to the hospital. It was then that I started to notice that his relapses occurred when his work life was unstable. I now know that having too much time on one's hands is dangerous for someone in recovery, but I didn't have that knowledge then. The treatment program at Hazelden was not the magic bullet I hoped it would be.

Fortunately, three months later, in March 2000, Ryan was hired full-time at another health care advertising agency, where he worked with a team of writers and artists on the design and execution of concepts for ad campaigns for different medications. He was completely engaged with his work, researching the efficacy and side effects of the drugs being touted for conditions such as Parkinson's disease, arthritis, sepsis, and hypertension. He was especially pleased to be working on a campaign for Lamictal, a new medication that was in pharmaceutical trials to treat bipolar disorder. Since he knew the condition from the inside, he thought he could design an ad that would visually demonstrate the experience of a patient with a mood disorder.

When I went to visit him that summer, he was in good spirits. He was proud of his work and eager to show me some of his computer drawings for the campaign. He had designed an ad with two people pulling a rope in a tug-of-war to demonstrate the struggle between mania and depression.

"I brought the rope in to work, and one of the women in the art department and I played tug-of-war so I could figure out the stance and body position of the players. See how hard it is to hold your position when you're off-balance?"

I could see what he meant. It was a very effective way to show the stress of the extreme mood swings a patient with bipolar disorder endures. An ad I liked even more was a pattern of footsteps in a loose circle on an implied pathway that demonstrated confusion and turmoil, sometimes going forward, sometimes going back. As I looked at his design, I could feel the uncertainty of those steps in my own body. It also struck me that those footsteps were a metaphor for my son's life.

* * *

Ryan kept the job at the ad agency for almost two years. He loved the work and was well compensated. He was taking his medication and said he was sober. This time, his forward momentum was interrupted abruptly not by his own behavior, but by tragic circumstances. When the World Trade Center was attacked on September 11, 2001, thousands of lives were lost in the Twin Towers and the lives of many of those who worked in Manhattan were irrevocably changed. Ryan's midtown office emptied out immediately after the Twin Towers were destroyed, and he, along with thousands of other people, walked out of Manhattan over the Fifty-Ninth Street Bridge, sharing water bottles, comforting one another, and giving directions about how to get home without the subway.

Amid the devastation of the attack on the city's security, the ad agency, like so many other businesses, started to disintegrate. It limped along with the sagging economy, downsized, and eventually moved its operations to New Jersey in a desperate attempt to survive. For months, Ryan commuted from Brooklyn to New Jersey and survived the weekly layoffs, but he was finally let go when the agency closed its doors in the beginning of 2002.

Ryan was at loose ends without the structure of his work schedule. At the time, he was also working on a sequence of paintings he called *The Heart Series*, and he tried to get a gallery show, without success. Two months after he left his job, he fell from the fire escape outside his apartment. He had lost his keys, and, as he had done previously in San Francisco, tried to break into his apartment through the window. This time, when he was taken to the hospital, he was considered a danger to himself. The doctors stapled his scalp together and kept him for observation in the psychiatric wing of Bellevue Hospital. He was treated for a week and then released on Depakote and Klonopin, medications he had taken before.

Unemployment insurance sustained him financially for the next year, but his bipolar condition and substance abuse problems worsened. Six months after his hospitalization, I got a call from Diana, who was aggravated and upset.

"I just came home from work, and Ryan's passed out on my couch. I think it's a heroin overdose. What do you want me to do?"

After she confirmed he was still breathing, I said, "Call an ambulance and tell them to take him to Bellevue. I don't know what else to do."

He was treated for eleven days for a manic episode and heroin relapse and then referred to addiction counseling. During that time, I was a wreck. I didn't know whether his repeated hospitalizations were a result of mania, drug abuse, or actual suicide attempts. He adamantly denied being suicidal, but the hospitalizations indicated that he was out of control.

While he was at Bellevue, I talked with him and the psychiatrist on call almost daily, but Ryan never revealed what had triggered this latest episode. Jerry flew back to New York to visit him and to talk with his friends, who by that time were tired of Ryan's emergencies disrupting their lives. With the help of colleagues in the addiction field, we were able to pave the way for his treatment in an outpatient dual-diagnosis program at St. Luke's Hospital in Manhattan.

I felt a need for help, too. My hands were tied with Ryan's constant denial about what was going on in his life coupled with the reality of his recurring hospitalizations. I contacted NAMI, the National Alliance on Mental Illness, and signed up for a course in Santa Barbara for family members of loved ones with mental illness.

* * *

NAMI's twelve-week Family-to-Family educational program was a godsend. It didn't alleviate my anxiety, but it gave me a lot of information about brain disorders and the effects of mental illness on a family. My class of fifteen was made up of parents, siblings, spouses, and adult children of parents who suffered from depression, bipolar illness, or schizophrenia. We had each weathered innumerable crises and had experienced phases of shock, denial, hope, anger, guilt, resentment, and grief. Until this workshop, none of us had reached the phases of understanding and acceptance of the illness. Most of us were in the middle of an emergency and didn't know what to do.

We learned that the person with a mental illness has lost control over their thoughts and feelings and is in an altered state of reality. When this occurs, most family members feel over-whelmed, confused, and at a loss for how to respond. Some meet each event with denial and refuse to believe it's happening. The pain is too intense to accept. They reject the facts despite over-whelming evidence to the contrary. Or they may think mental illness is a phase that will pass. They "normalize" the situation with such bromides as "it's part of growing up," "boys will be boys," and "he'll get over it." I had a similar reaction when Ryan's depression occurred in college when I convinced myself he might just be having "sophomore-year blues."

Other family members become heroic. They do everything possible to help their loved one in crisis, in an attempt to bring them back from the hell of their illness. When they recognize that the serious problems are not going away, they assume that if they make an even *bigger* effort, things will change and everything will return to normal. This approach often involves a significant outlay of money; no expense is too big for these family members, even if it means taking a second job or depleting their savings. One of the reasons I took the job in Santa Barbara was that I was told I could put Ryan on my health insurance. This turned out not to be true: after I took the job, I was told he was too old to be considered a dependent.

The hope-against-hope stage is part of a family member's nature. In times of crisis, we all yearn for a return to what we considered "normal." I contacted everyone I knew in the mental health and addiction fields to find just the "right" treatment for Ryan, hoping the next one would help him get well. In spite of having a good job, I often needed to borrow additional money from family members for these expensive, uninsurable treatments. In that regard, I have been fortunate. I know families who don't have financial support and feel powerless when their mentally ill or drug-addicted adult child ends up on the streets because our system does not serve them.

I began to understand that there is no perfect treatment. A brain disorder is unpredictable; it can be managed for a period of time with medication, but it does not go away. When our loved one has another crisis or another relapse, we feel angry and resentful and ask, "How could this happen again?" The subtler message is, "How could he/she do this to me?" We blame the person with the mental illness and want them to "snap out of it."

I heard that phrase many times at family meetings, particularly from fathers who had a difficult time accepting that their child was mentally ill. Alternately, mothers often feel enormous guilt that somehow it is their fault their child is ill and suffering.

For some of us, including me, the reaction is to get overinvolved with the problem. I often observed myself being simultaneously angry and caring toward Ryan. Then I felt schizoid because of the mixed messages I was sending him.

When we finally acknowledge that our loved one has a catastrophic illness, it is not unusual to mark time before and after the defining event—the first psychotic break. We mourn the loss of the person we knew and loved before the illness struck, because we know they will never be that person again. We begin to feel the deep tragedy of their lives, as well as our own, because our dreams for them have been dashed. Our grief over this loss never disappears. In NAMI, the term for this feeling is "chronic sorrow."

In class, we were encouraged to accept that bad things do happen to good people. We were asked to turn our anger and grief toward working for better care for the mentally ill and fighting the stigma of mental illness that shames both patients and their families. At the time, none of us was ready to move into advocacy, but it was good to know that at some point we might progress to that stage.

Most of us went to the weekly meetings to understand the symptoms of mental illness, to find out about treatment, to learn coping tools, and for support. In dealing with a crisis, we were encouraged to stay calm, trust our intuition about when to get help, and practice skills about setting limits, avoiding confrontation, and communicating clearly. The most comforting information I received from the course was, "We did not cause the mental illness. We cannot cure it. We cannot control it. We can only learn to cope with it." Living with a mental illness ultimately teaches humility and compassion not only for our loved one but also for ourselves.

Learning about the specific symptoms of bipolar illness began to demystify the disorder for me and helped me both to understand and to have compassion for what Ryan experienced, particularly during his manic episodes. It was important to me to sort out how much of his illness was due to bipolar disorder and how much of it was due to substance abuse. Now, it seems naive, but I still thought that if he could get the right treatment and be put on the correct medication, he wouldn't need to use illegal drugs to alleviate his symptoms. This is the desperate hope against hope many family members experience. I didn't understand that approximately 80 percent of people with bipolar illness also have a substance abuse problem. The NAMI course did not deal in any depth with the issue of substance abuse. At that time, it was still seen as separate from mental illness. The moral stigma associated with substance abuse prevented the two from being seen as a treatable coexisting disorder.

As I listened to the stories of other members of the class, I came to realize there was no way to separate the dual nature of bipolar illness and addiction. Because there are different, and sometimes conflicting, philosophies about and treatment approaches for substance abuse and mental illness, there is still very little integration of the two. I found myself both confused and frustrated by my lack of clarity about how to treat Ryan's problems.

chapter 8

leaving new york

Ryan's friends and his girlfriend, Diana, were having difficulty coping with Ryan's crises. In two years, they'd had to deal with his burned foot, his fall from his fire escape, and a heroin overdose. They had given him enormous support and love during his two hospitalizations, visiting him, cheering him on, and keeping Jerry and me in the loop. Unfortunately, his inability to keep his promises to them about abstinence wore thin. They went through the same roller coaster cycles of fear, hope, and disappointment we had been going through for years, only they had a lower tolerance level for them. His final hospitalization at Bellevue was a turning point for Diana. She told me by phone that she no longer wanted to be responsible for Ryan's safety and encouraged Jerry and me to bring him back to the West Coast.

It was difficult for us to decide what to do because Jerry and I were in different stages of understanding about Ryan's illness.

I had sent Jerry NAMI literature, but he was not interested in attending meetings. Even though he had seen Ryan in the hospital, he still thought Ryan's main problem was immaturity. He wanted him to "snap out of it and grow up." He denied the impact of the illness on the deterioration of Ryan's life. I wanted to find a West Coast doctor who specialized in dual diagnosis, and I also thought Ryan would benefit from family support. It took us months to agree on a plan and then more time to persuade Ryan to leave New York. In the end, he agreed only because his landlord evicted him.

Different philosophies about dealing with a loved one with an addiction problem—in our case, a son—can cause chaos in a family. Proponents of the zero tolerance/tough love approach say, "don't support him, don't give him any money, let him hit bottom, and he'll bounce back up in time and recover on his own." By some accounts, 35 percent of people with substance abuse problems do recover independently, meaning they stop using and start living productive lives.

An alternative approach, "harm reduction," cautions that addicts don't bounce; they either splat or get used to living at the bottom, and the bottom keeps getting deeper. This approach looks at the bio-psychosocial factors that contribute to drug use. The next step is to come up with a plan for how to decrease use of the addictive substance, with the intention of bringing less harm to the user and their family. The ultimate goal is harm reduction.

When Jerry and I were trying to figure out what to do, I heard arguments from addiction specialists for both points of view. At times Jerry argued for giving Ryan the opportunity to hit bottom and test his resiliency. He believed Ryan had it in him to bounce back and take control of his life. I considered addiction a problem of brain chemistry, not an issue of faulty will-power or poor morals, and thought it inhumane to let someone with a mental illness flail on their own. I was afraid that Ryan was too exhausted from repeated episodes of illness to bounce back. I was scared he would hit bottom and splat.

Ryan's life was completely out of control. He had just completed an outpatient drug treatment program at St. Luke's in Manhattan, but he didn't have a job, his girlfriend had left him, and his friends were pulling away. I was paying for his psychiatric care, and Jerry was paying his rent. It didn't look like Ryan was going to be able to get a job anytime soon. Trying to get his life back on track in New York seemed improbable. Jerry suggested that Ryan live near him and generously offered Ryan a job doing legal research with him in Los Angeles.

It sounded like a positive solution. He could start a new life, develop an alternative professional skill, leave the temptations of his neighborhood in Brooklyn, and deepen his relationship with his father. I was relieved when Ryan agreed to the plan, not only because he would have Jerry's immediate physical and emotional support but because, I imagined, it would allow me to be less emotionally involved.

By that time, I was exhausted by Ryan's cycles of illness and reckless behavior. Every time the phone rang, I was terrified I was going to learn of another hospitalization or something worse. At times, I didn't feel as if I had a life separate from his. I was in a constant state of anxiety and grief. I also felt enormous guilt about his suffering and my inability to find the right solution to his illness. I also felt enormous admiration for Ryan's courage. I could not have weathered the indignities of his condition as well as he did. He never gave up. He always picked himself up from the latest calamity and went on. His spirit was strong. I loved my son.

Still, like many mothers, I felt I had carried the major responsibility, both financial and emotional, since Ryan had first been diagnosed. I wanted someone else to accept the responsibility for a while. It didn't immediately happen. With a ticking eviction notice for the end of June, Ryan still procrastinated leaving Brooklyn.

After five years, I had recently resigned from my teaching post in Santa Barbara and moved to the Bay Area to be with my new partner, Bill, and near my daughter. Bill and I had met briefly twenty years before with our respective spouses and had been reintroduced by my friend Connie, who thought I needed a man I could count on. She was right in her choice for me. I flew back to New York in June to help Ryan pack and move back to the West Coast.

Ryan was living in the Williamsburg section of Brooklyn, in an area filled with family-owned Italian delis and pastry shops. He loved the neighborhood and the friendliness of the local merchants and knew the intimacy of this ethnic community did not exist in Santa Monica. However, his affection for his neighborhood was not reflected in his abhorrent living conditions. His third-floor walk-up studio apartment mirrored his disheveled mental state. There was oil paint covered with a layer of dust on the walls around the paintings he was working on. To get his security deposit back, we spent days scraping the old paint off the walls and scrubbing the hardwood floors. It was ninety-eight degrees outside and even hotter inside. Our tempers flared as I tried to get him to sort through books, computer files, CDs, artwork, music, clothes, and unpaid bills. Bill, who happened to be visiting his own daughter in Manhattan, volunteered to help us on the final day to organize, pack, label, and catalog the contents of thirty-two boxes. Two men from UPS came and loaded them onto their truck and shipped them off to Santa Monica.

While I was on my hands and knees, scrubbing Ryan's floor, I wondered how life had evolved to this point. I thought back to a conversation Ryan and I had twenty-three years earlier, when he was thirteen. The occasion was my father's retirement party. Ryan, Liz, and I had flown in from Los Angeles to join in the festivities. With the glow of the Manhattan skyline beside us, we were standing on the front deck of the Circle Line ship, cruising down the Hudson River toward the Statue of Liberty.

Ryan said, "Dad wants me to come and live with him."

Staring out at the lights, I could barely comprehend his words. "He what?"

"Dad wants me to come and live with him."

I thought, *How come Jerry has never mentioned this to me?*

"When?" I asked.

"As soon as possible. At the end of summer vacation, before school starts."

My heart started pounding. My head got light. I panicked and started to cry. "Do you want to go?"

Silence.

"I don't want you to go."

I couldn't believe I was saying that. I became so emotional and muttered everything at once. I didn't want to lose him—not yet, at thirteen. I didn't want him to leave me. I didn't want him to live with his father. He never broached the subject again. Nor did I ever ask Jerry about it. Ryan continued to live with me until he left for college.

As I scraped the paint off the hardwood floor, I wondered if things would have been different, even better for him, had he gone to live with his dad. Now, through terrible circumstances, he would have an opportunity to find that out.

* * *

For two months, things went smoothly for Ryan in Santa Monica. Jerry found him an apartment near his house and bought him a used car, and Ryan began to learn new skills as a paralegal. Ryan liked working with his dad and earning his approval. He also reconnected with some of his boyhood friends, many now married and starting families. I found him a local psychiatrist who was doing cutting-edge research on bipolar illness for the National Institute of Mental Health. She began to treat Ryan with Lamictal, the very drug for which he had designed an ad campaign. He liked her and seemed to adjust well to the new medication.

Then, coming home one night from visiting a friend, he sideswiped a parked car. Police arrived and found a small amount of cocaine under his passenger seat. Ryan denied any knowledge of the coke but was charged with possession. His denial did not convince his dad or me, but because I had no knowledge of Ryan's having used coke before, I convinced myself it was possible that it belonged to someone else. When he blamed the roommate of the friend he had visited, I believed him. I desperately wanted this new opportunity with his father to turn his life around. I was also terrified he would be convicted of a felony.

His dad was in no mood to help him get legal counsel, despite being a lawyer himself. He was tired of Ryan's crises. Ryan got himself a public defender. When he appeared before the judge two months later, because he was a first offender, his case was diverted out of the criminal system into drug court under Proposition 36. He had to satisfy the requirements of outpatient treatment in order for his criminal record to be expunged. Ryan continued to work for his dad and attended classes in drug relapse prevention at night. He was drug tested weekly. Despite this crisis, I thought that once Ryan fulfilled his treatment requirements, his life would stabilize.

Soon after he finished the mandated treatment, he started to show signs of depression. He was having difficulty sleeping and periodically missed work. He was also having problems getting along with his father's wife. Because his behavior was erratic, including sometimes nodding off in the middle of a family dinner, his stepmother didn't want him in their home around her nine-year-old son.

One spring morning, Jerry went to Ryan's apartment to find out why he had missed work. He found Ryan unconscious, facedown on his bed. Ryan had taken a mixture of cocaine, chloral hydrate, and codeine to put himself to sleep. The paramedics rushed him to the hospital, and it took several hours to bring him around. He was transferred to the psych ward at Los Angeles County+USC Medical Center for a "medical overdose." Sitting in the locked ward, Ryan was adamant in our phone conversation that he was not trying to take his life.

"I just needed a rest, Mom," he said. "Don't worry. I didn't want to kill myself. If I had, I've saved enough pills; I wouldn't have failed."

chapter 9

the late thirties

Three weeks after Ryan's hospitalization, I flew to Santa Monica to discuss next steps with him and Jerry. I arrived late at our meeting spot, a Mexican restaurant called Gilbert's, and found Ryan and Jerry waiting in the parking lot.

I hadn't seen Ryan and his father together since Ryan's seizure seven years earlier. They were both handsome. Ryan might not have inherited his father's height, but he had the shape of his father's face and his chiseled cheekbones. And while Jerry and I had not been together in many years, we were s sstill connected by our concern for our son.

"We can't eat here; it's too crowded," Jerry said. "And we can't have this meeting; it's too late. I have a client at three thirty."

"What do you mean, we can't have this meeting? We have to have this meeting. We'll find another place to eat." To Ryan's dismay, we settled on a nearby McDonald's.

"I'm not going into McDonald's," he said. I ignored him.

I wanted this meeting to discuss plans for Ryan's health care. Jerry and I had a contentious relationship, but we both agreed Ryan needed residential treatment. For the first time in twenty-six years, he and I sat next to each other. It was a strange sensation, sitting together in a McDonald's booth, facing our son, who, despite telling us that he had not eaten in three days, adamantly refused to order anything but a milk shake. I pulled out a file of papers and spread them on the table, determined to begin the conversation that none of us wanted to have.

"Ryan, I put together a list of your ten hospitalizations over the last sixteen years. All of them were precipitated by drug overdoses. Your dad and I want you to go into a residential rehab program now. We don't see any alternative."

"I'm not going into any program with a bunch of loonies again," he said. "I'm in AA and that's enough."

"Dad's willing to take you to check out Azusa's Rehab Treatment program, or other programs like Colonial House or Phoenix House. We've exhausted all other remedies. I'm not even sure you're bipolar."

My words felt harsh, but I was stunned by the frequency of his medical overdoses. Did Ryan treat his mood episodes by self-medicating, or had his early diagnosis of bipolar illness become a foil for drug addiction? There was some truth in both. Either way, I was sick of his merry-go-round of ineffective treatment.

"I don't know if I'm bipolar either," Ryan said, "but I do know I've got a good AA meeting, I have a sponsor, and I don't want to go to some lockup desert rehab, particularly in the summer." His comment about not wanting to go to someplace hot reminded me that when he first asked for help, he didn't want to go someplace cold either. His resistance had an interesting pattern.

It struck me that AA might be enough for some people, but it certainly didn't seem like enough for Ryan. "You've tried AA before," I said. "What do you think is going to be different this time? How are you different?"

"AA works in mysterious ways. I can't guarantee that things will be different. I won't promise I'll stay sober. I can take things only one day at a time. If I went to Azusa, what would I do when I got out, anyway? Where would I go?"

Jerry interjected, "When people finish treatment there, Azusa helps them with job placement and housing."

"I'm not going. It's a waste of money. You sent me to Hazelden, and I hated it. This will be worse."

I wanted to respond that Hazelden had helped him stay clean and sober for two years, but Jerry cut me off. He shook his head and got up to leave.

"Then there's nothing more to say," he said.

I turned to Ryan, panicked. Once again, I had hoped that if Ryan saw his parents united in their concern for him, he'd agree to residential treatment. Without it, I feared, he'd end up homeless on the street.

"Would you at least think about it?" I said. "Your dad and I can't continue to support you."

To keep Ryan safe, for the past three weeks Jerry had been sleeping on the floor of Ryan's studio apartment. Finding Ryan unconscious had shaken Jerry. If he hadn't found him, Ryan would have been dead. But, understandably, Jerry had now run out of patience.

"We're serious about cutting you off financially," said Jerry. "After this month, I'm not going to pay your rent."

"There are other people who love me who will help me out," Ryan said.

He sounded like a six-year-old. When Jerry asked him who, Ryan mentioned Michael, a friend in the Bay Area, who had himself lost his job because of health issues and needed someone to care for him.

"Michael said I can live with him."

"What does he live on?" asked Jerry.

"Disability insurance," Ryan said.

"Doesn't sound like he'll be able to help you out much."

"No, but he said I could live with him. I could take care of him, and he could help me put together my résumé to find work."

I could hardly imagine my son taking care of anybody else.

"Think about Azusa," I said.

"He won't," said Jerry. "He wants it his own way."

"You don't know anything about me," Ryan said.

We fell silent and waited.

"I'll go look at it with you," Ryan said, without looking up from the table.

"Then I'll make arrangements," said Jerry.

They visited Azusa three days later. When Ryan was informed there was no psychiatrist on staff and the patient population consisted primarily of young men, he refused to go.

* * *

Ryan continued to work part-time for his dad, but Jerry refused to continue to pay his rent. Ryan found a job designing a new magazine dedicated to work environments through his new girlfriend, Joyce, a writer and editor there. They worked around the clock to get the magazine into production.

Three months after our McDonald's meeting, I met Ryan at his Santa Monica apartment. Like his disheveled studio in Williamsburg, it mirrored his lack of attention to his personal life. He hadn't washed the dishes: Top Ramen stuck to the bottom of his lone saucepan, and an open box of Total perched on top of his pile of phone bills, next to the brief he was working on for his dad. Hospital and ambulance bills were neatly stacked in their unopened envelopes on the floor. There was no place to sit on the worn leather couch because it was covered with newspapers, *New Yorker*s, and notices from creditors. He hadn't unpacked half of the thirty-two boxes we had shipped from Brooklyn the year before. They rose up in the corner of the room like a totem pole narrating his history. A pile of his *Heart Series* paintings leaned precariously on top of a shorter stack of boxes.

Ryan dressed like a high school kid: baggy black pants, an oversize red T-shirt, a black jacket, black-and-white Keds, and a black baseball cap pulled low over his forehead. He was animated and looked healthier. We walked to Lucy's restaurant on Pico.

I was eager to hear how he planned to raise the rest of his rent money to avoid eviction. His sister had sent him $200 she could not afford. At Lucy's, he presented me with the first issue of *Workspace*.

"Here it is, Mom. Hot off the press."

He was the creative director for this issue, and the design was impressive.

"This is gorgeous," I said. "I had no idea it would have such heft. Congratulations."

"Yeah, the publisher has been getting a lot of positive feedback, but he didn't invite me to work on the next issue. He doesn't want to spend the money to do it right—he wants to use interns instead."

My ears pricked. It was always someone else's fault when a job didn't work out. I watched him work his charm on the waitress as he placed his order.

Then I asked what he was going to do about rent.

"I got a job in a car wash starting tomorrow."

"What are you going to do there?"

"I'll work behind the counter as a cashier, but I hope to get on the line, washing cars. It's a high-end place that details cars, and I've been told the customers give good tips."

I was both surprised and pleased he had found a job, but that didn't mitigate my anxiety about the prospect of his homelessness. Before I could go on, he changed the subject. "Mom, look at that guy working on his laptop. It looks like he's designing toilet bowls."

Sure enough, the man was working on a design for a toilet bowl. Ryan had always been unusually observant, but all I wanted to talk about was logistics.

"How are you going to handle your rent situation?"

"I gave the manager the two hundred dollars Liz sent me, but I need another nine hundred dollars to be current. If you could spare seven hundred, I can get the rest from Dad. He owes me money for some research I did for him. We're working on a really complicated legal case."

I pushed my full plate away from me. I couldn't eat.

"What do you mean, *spare* seven hundred dollars?"

"I just thought you could lend it to me until I get another job."

"I don't think you realize that you're being evicted from

your apartment. You have to find a cheaper place to live. I can write you a check this time, but then what happens? I can't keep bailing you out. You've got to find a place you can afford."

He said nothing but continued to eat his omelet. I waited for his response. It was getting late, and I'd have to leave for the class I was teaching at UCLA. I knew we would not resolve anything that morning. Instead, I did what I had done so many times before. I took out my checkbook and wrote a check to the realty company that managed his apartment complex. I handed it to him.

"Thanks. I'll pay you back," he said. He put the check in a ripped envelope in his pile of papers. My cell phone rang; it was my sister.

"Rosemary, I'll have to talk to you later. I'm in a meeting with Ryan, and we have to get some things sorted out."

"No, no, let me talk to her," Ryan said, and grabbed the cell phone away from me. He joked with her on the phone as I paid for our breakfast.

We left Lucy's, and he continued to talk with my sister as we walked up the street to his apartment.

"I could come and live with you," he said to her, joking. "With Juli and Cristin away at college, you have lots of empty rooms. You've always said you wanted a son, right? You're my godmother; you're supposed to take care of me. No, not just my spiritual well-being!"

I grabbed the phone.

"He's really on a roll, isn't he?" said my sister, laughing.

"Yeah, but it's not so funny. I'll call you later."

The conversation between them was crazy making. I didn't know whether he was cycling up in a manic phase or was high. Once again, he had avoided talking about next steps in his life.

"Why don't you take the check to the apartment manager now?" I asked.

Ryan looked for the check in the papers he was carrying. Then he went through all of his pockets. No check. Even though I knew I had just given it to him, I went through my own pockets, my purse, and my checkbook.

We were both sweating as we got down on our knees on the hard pavement, still looking for the check. Cars beeped and jackhammers rang. All of a sudden, Ryan took off down the street, running toward Lucy's, letting all his papers blow in the wind. I gathered them up and waited in my car. He came back after several minutes. The check had vanished into thin air.

* * *

This interaction between my son and me made me think of my mother's mother, Grandmother Dunn, dead at age one hundred, nine years earlier. She, too, had a son who suffered from an addiction. Uncle Joe was a parish priest in New York and an alcoholic. Every summer when I was a little girl, I spent a week with Nana and my grandfather Poppy. I loved going to their house in Rego Park, a mostly Irish American blue-collar neighborhood in Queens. Every row house had lace curtains on the front parlor windows. Each morning, Nana and I would go to the butcher, baker, and fishmonger and then home so she could begin to cook. I'd sit in the kitchen and watch her prepare an elaborate lunch for Uncle Joe, who would be arriving soon.

One particularly hot and humid day when I was six, I sat at the bottom of the stairs, waiting for my uncle's arrival. I had a panoramic view from my perch. I could see the parlor in the front of the house to my left, the dining room in front of me, and the kitchen to my right.

Uncle Joe entered wearing his priest's collar and black suit. He was sweating. "Hi, Ma. It sure is hot outside."

He was handsome, with thick black hair and dark eyebrows, and cheerful, and always ready with a story or a quick joke. He made people laugh. Nana was thrilled to see him.

"I have your lunch ready, Joe," she sang out from the kitchen. She walked into the dining room and raised her arms to give him a hug, revealing the loose flesh of her pale white arm. He hugged her back and gave her a kiss.

"You look as beautiful as ever, Ma," he said. That's when she pushed him away.

"You've been drinking," she hollered in a tone that scared me. "I can smell it on your breath."

"Oh, Ma, I just had a quick one with some of the guys down at the fire station. I'm fine."

"You're not fine," she shot back. "What are you doing, drinking so early? It's not even midday. Drinking, and probably with a woman. It's that Helen, isn't it?"

"No, Ma, there's no woman. I just had a quick drink with Pat down at the station. Now, what did you make me for lunch? It smells like clam chowder."

She turned on her heel and stalked into the kitchen. He followed her.

"I knew it—look at this!" said Uncle Joe, as he picked up the lid on the pot on the stove. "You know I love your clam chowder. You're a marvel."

Her frown loosened. He put his arm around her and gave

her a squeeze. She relaxed. He took off his collar and jacket and put them on the back of a chair.

"I was able to get some fresh clams this morning when Meg and I went to the fish market," she said.

Neither one of them had noticed me sitting on the stairs. I observed their exchange from the dining room. Nana brought him a bowl of her Manhattan clam chowder. I walked into the kitchen.

"Now, where were you hiding?" he exclaimed, as he pulled me to him and gave me a big hug. I smelled the liquor on his breath. There was something exciting—perhaps forbidden— about its sweet smell. Why did it make my grandmother mad?

That scene in Rego Park over fifty years ago was a scenario that repeated over and over, each time I went to visit. Nana spent the morning preparing a special lunch for Uncle Joe. He walked into the house like he owned it. He never knocked or called out to announce his arrival. She always acted as if a suitor had come to woo her. Uncle Joe was God, her ticket into heaven. He would embrace her, she would smell liquor on his breath, and then she would get angry. Again.

Their routine never varied. He brushed off her anger and jollied her up with some yarn or compliment, and she relented, silently forgiving him while she fed him. The similarity of the scene with my son at Lucy's was not lost on me. Ryan's charm could easily distract me from confronting him or staying angry.

For a long time, Uncle Joe's charm ameliorated my grandmother's spirits and soothed her worried soul. But then things got out of control. He had several car accidents, was charged with drunk driving, fell and broke his hip, and was removed from successive parishes. Nana was ashamed. She went to Mass every day to pray for her son and continued to serve him lunch. Her tongue-lashings became more severe. Years later, the archdiocese sent Uncle Joe away to "take the cure." After several such sojourns, it took; he joined AA and was given a new parish. Now, I seemed to be reenacting my grandmother's cycles of a mother's hope, disappointment, shame, and despair.

chapter 10

endocarditis—everything changed

A few weeks later, something much more serious eclipsed Ryan's housing concerns and financial woes. A week after he started working at the car wash, Jerry took him to the emergency room with a 103-degree fever. At first, the doctors sent him home with antibiotics, but when the fever didn't break after five days, he was admitted to St. John's Hospital, where he was diagnosed with endocarditis. Apparently, one-third of the patients who contract this life-threatening bacterial infection of the lining of the heart have abused street drugs. I visited him several times during the first weeks he was in the intensive care unit; I was terrified he was not going to survive.

He was kept on intravenous antibiotics for a month, until he started to stabilize. At that point, Rita, the hospital's social worker, arranged a meeting with Ryan and his five doctors to discuss his illness and plans for future treatment. She asked that Jerry, Liz, and I attend as well. She wanted us all to hear their recommendations.

In early October, we gathered, along with Ryan's girlfriend, Joyce, in the small "family room" on the fourth floor of the hospital. Ryan walked in, attached to an ambulatory IV drip, wearing white-and-blue-print hospital-issue pajama bottoms and the gray sweatshirt Liz and I had bought for him the night before. His face was pale, and he was sweating. He sat in a chair on the other side of the room, across from the family.

The doctors filed in at 7:00 A.M. and sat down together on the same side of the room as Ryan. After introductions, the infectious-disease expert, Dr. Murphy, said she was concerned because Ryan's temperature had spiked during the night. I mentioned that my daughter and I had accompanied Ryan outside the front door of the hospital the night before for fresh air and I hoped he hadn't caught a chill.

Dr. Murphy's face turned red. "That wouldn't cause a spike in his temp," she said. Then she looked at us and snapped. "I don't trust you, I don't trust you, and I don't trust you," she said, pointing her index finger in turn at me, Liz, and Joyce. She looked at Ryan and then turned back to face me. "He knows he can't leave the floor. And you know better, too."

I told her no one had told us he was restricted to his floor and that his nurse had known we were going out for a few minutes. Joyce added that the internist sitting next to Dr. Murphy had recently told Ryan to get some fresh air.

"Well, I don't know anything about that," Dr. Murphy insisted. "I don't know any of you, but it's clear to me he's been manipulating all of you for years, and he's not going to manipulate me!"

The harshness of her tone was alarming.

"He might sneak downstairs to the hospital fountain and

meet a drug dealer, like one of my other patients did, who died on my watch. That is not going to happen to me again."

At the time, her accusations seemed outrageous. Yes, Ryan's heart condition was the result of his intravenous drug use, but it was still too painful for me to accept that he was a habitual user. She left no time for a response and was on to the next item on her agenda. She used the back of a piece of paper to sketch and show us an elementary drawing of the human heart.

"Your son has a fairly large bacterial growth on his right heart valve, and abscesses, like scabs that have sloughed off from the growth, have lodged in his lungs and kidneys. The staph is very resistant to treatment."

Seeing the confused looks on our faces, she added, "Not the staff in the hospital, the staphylococcus that has attacked his kidneys. We're consulting with the CDC [Centers for Disease Control and Prevention] to find out if this is a new, virulent strain of staph. If he continues not to respond to the antibiotic, we have no other options because we've tried everything else."

She gestured to the cardiac surgeon, who reminded me of a butcher in photographer August Sander's startling black-and-white portraits of German workers from the 1940s. His chest was broad, his hands beefy, and I trusted he could crack open a heart cavity with the flick of his wrist.

"I won't know how much damage has been done to his heart valve until I open him up," he said. "If it is extensive, which I think it is, the heart valve will have to be replaced with a mechanical one, and he'll have to be on Coumadin for the rest of his life." He addressed Ryan directly as Ryan crossed his arms in front of his chest and looked down at the floor.

"The Coumadin will have to be monitored weekly by a doctor and scheduled in such a way that it does not interfere with your other medications. There are side effects to taking a blood thinner. If you fall and hit your head, you could have bleeding inside your brain. If we don't have to replace the heart valve with a mechanical one, I could give you a pig valve and you wouldn't have to take the blood thinner. But, as I said, I won't know until I open you up.

"You have to decide whether you're willing to have surgery. You're a young man; I suggest getting it done now, instead of having another incident and coming in three years from now. And if you ever use another street drug, you'll drop dead."

During the four weeks Ryan had been in the hospital, all of his doctors had repeatedly emphasized the danger involved in his continued use of street drugs. Yet Ryan sat there impassively. His expression seemed to indicate both his disdain for their constant hammering and his denial. The night before this meeting, I had met with the pain control specialist and told him Ryan was still complaining about discomfort from the abscesses in his lumbar area. I asked why the specialist wasn't giving Ryan something stronger to manage his pain. "He can have all the methadone he wants for pain," the doctor said, "but he is always going to complain about pain. That's the nature of his illness."

"Which illness are you talking about?" I asked, not knowing whether he was referring to Ryan's psychiatric illness or to his heart disease.

"His bipolar disorder, as well as his problems with addiction. He wants something strong, like morphine, to give him a high, and I'm not going to give it to him. We're trying to keep him from hurting himself."

I had never before heard a health professional say that Ryan's addiction was so out of control that he was incapable of protecting himself from self-destruction. My worst fears about his drug abuse were being confirmed. In hindsight, I see that all the signs that Ryan could hurt himself were there. He had already been self-destructing for a decade.

"Does the methadone do anything to alleviate the pain?"

"Absolutely. It works by slowly and steadily decreasing the pain. The problem is that he wants something that gives him a sense of euphoria. He was asking for all kinds of drugs when he came in here. He was totally inappropriate with the staff."

My heart sank. I was embarrassed for my son and for myself. I asked the doctor if they had done a toxicology screening on Ryan. He confirmed that there had been cocaine in his system, although Ryan had denied using any street drugs since his last "accidental overdose."

I felt like a fool. I had told the doctor at the ICU that Ryan had been clean for four months. "Oh, four months?" she had said with surprise in a thick Brooklyn accent, shaking her head. "Is that what he told you? They usually say they've been clean for a year. I've never heard four months before." The word "they" pierced my heart. She had just thrown my son in with all the other addicts with endocarditis.

At the group meeting, the psychiatrist spoke last. He sat apart from the other doctors and spoke directly to Ryan: "When you're released, we want you to go into a drug rehab program. We're all concerned that you're going to have difficulty functioning outside. I don't think you'll be able to handle the daily stresses on your own or to enter an intense treatment program. We want you to start a four-hour-a-day outpatient program."

Ryan said nothing.

The psychiatrist continued, "I also want to make sure you don't get too depressed. I know it's hard sitting in a hospital bed week after week, waiting to get better. I think it would be good if you could go outside for a breath of fresh air from time to time, with supervision." He looked at his colleagues. "We'll have to have a meeting about how to manage that."

Of the doctors assembled, he had the most empathy for my son's condition. I appreciated his tone. He didn't try to shame us.

Ryan finally spoke. His voice was strong as he addressed the psychiatrist. "I have a problem with how my psych meds are being administered. I'm being given them at different times than when I take them on the outside, and I can't sleep."

The psychiatrist nodded. "We can certainly adjust the scheduling of your meds. I don't know who decided how they were to be administered when you came in." He turned to Jerry.

"Don't look at me. I just told the doctor what meds he was taking when we came into the ER. That was over a month ago."

As I glanced at Jerry, it struck me that we were both so terrified we were going to lose Ryan that we had reached some level of equanimity with each other.

The meeting ended with Rita, the social worker, telling Ryan, "You're not doing a very good job of taking care of yourself. You expect everyone to do everything for you."

Her bluntness, the cardiac surgeon's directness about the surgery Ryan needed, and Dr. Murphy's shaming of the family collided inside me. I felt as if a semi had just mowed me down. Paradoxically, I appreciated that Dr. Murphy had laid bare the results of my son's addiction. I thanked her. She nodded. The doctors filed out of the meeting, leaving the family to ponder all that had been said.

"You certainly have a team committed to your healing," I said to Ryan, trying to hold back my tears. I hadn't looked at him much during the meeting, except when he'd talked about his medication. "What did you think of the meeting?"

He didn't look at me. "I didn't hear anything new," he said. "I've heard everything they said before."

He seemed totally unaffected. He showed no fear, no sadness, no shame. My heart sank. Nothing was going to change. A life-threatening illness was not enough to scare him. He looked up and said to no one in particular, "I'm not having the surgery."

* * *

On the six-hour drive back to the Bay Area with Liz, I couldn't stop crying. I was both bereft and livid, and Liz was tired of Ryan's dramas. She was sick of the attention he got and the effect his crises had on me. The entire time Ryan was in the hospital, my terror that he was going to die kept me awake at night. When I did sleep, I had nightmares about his heart bursting open.

Two years before, I had bought one of the paintings in his *Heart Series*, an abstract that resembled a heart, a kidney, and a skull. The texture of the paint was rough and layered, like the inside of his organs, and his stark portrayal of the skull repulsed me. I had bought the painting because he needed the money at the time. Now the image had come to life: his heart and kidneys were infected, and he was wasting away.

We had already been dealing with his mental illness for sixteen years, and now we'd been told he had a heart condition caused by his injection of drugs. *His injection of drugs*. I was fed up with his refusal of addiction treatment. I wondered whether his mental illness had eradicated all insight about what he was doing to himself. Or perhaps he was so depressed that he was incapable of making a decision that would contribute to his health. Or maybe he was getting too much pleasure out of the drug life to stop. These unanswered questions continued to gnaw at me.

Growing up in an alcoholic family, I was used to living with murky suppositions about unanswered questions. There was always a fog in my home when there wasn't an eruption of violence or plates being smashed. As a child, I was frustrated with and scared by my father's refusal to deal with my mother's drinking. Now, as a mother, I was afraid that my son's refusal to get treatment for his own addiction was going to kill him. *Why can't we take care of this?* I thought. *Why can't he see what he's doing to himself—and to us?* I felt totally manipulated.

True to her word, Dr. Murphy kept Ryan in the hospital, on intravenous antibiotics, for another month. Rita was unable to find a facility for him to recuperate after his hospitalization; no local convalescent home would accept him, because of his drug history. Jerry had already terminated Ryan's apartment lease and moved his belongings into storage. He had nowhere to live.

According to Dr. Murphy, Ryan needed at least another two months of recuperation. Bill and I discussed the possibility of Ryan's staying with us temporarily on our rented houseboat in Sausalito. Bill was about to retire and had been looking forward to the freedom that would bring, yet he also had a desire to help Ryan restore his physical health, get back on his feet, live independently, and get a job. Bill had also accepted that Ryan's illness was part of our relationship. Years later, when I asked him why he put up with the chaos Ryan brought into our lives, he said,

"When we first started going out, Ryan's addiction wasn't a factor in our relationship and I wasn't going to leave you when life became difficult. I wanted to support Ryan's healing and at the same time, keep our relationship strong."

Ryan arrived in time for Thanksgiving.

chapter 11

the *pietà*

Each night after dinner on the houseboat, Ryan put on his bulky winter parka with the faux fur–trimmed hood and walked outside onto our pier to call his girlfriend, Joyce, in Los Angeles. "I can't get reception inside the houseboat," he explained.

There wasn't much for him to do while recuperating. He called his girlfriend and walked over to the liquor store and back nightly to report on the grizzled characters who hung out there. "They're a scary bunch," he said.

What about them scared him? Hadn't he seen similar unshaven characters in his travels scoring dope in New York and downtown Los Angeles? I had seen the look guys walking down the street in San Francisco's Mission district gave him; there was something they recognized in one another: a hunger, a desperation.

I didn't ask him much about anything because my therapist, Mike, told me to stop asking questions—questions about how he was feeling, how he was sleeping, whether he wanted the drawing table set up in his room, and when he would be coming back from a friend's house in the city.

Instead, shortly after he moved in with us, I took him to weekly chiropractor appointments or to have his blood drawn to make sure the bacterial infection in his heart and kidneys did not recur. I sent for his birth certificate from Philadelphia so he could complete his Social Security disability insurance (SSDI) application, and I paid his bills. He slept on and off most of the day, and the rest of the time, we all tried to give each other space. There was no dialogue about next steps or what he wanted from his life. Mike said what Ryan needed in order to heal was love, not prying.

Dr. Bea, our chiropractor, was encouraged by his progress. "Ryan has enormous healing potential," she told me the third week of his treatments. She mentioned that he was getting much stronger in spite of all he'd been through. I clung to her words.

He hadn't been interested in therapy, AA meetings, addiction counseling, or drawing, but he did keep all of his appointments with Dr. Bea, who gave him the most relief from his physical, and perhaps his emotional, suffering.

During Ryan's convalescence, my friend Hillary asked me a provocative question: "Does Ryan ask for your help, or do you always show up?"

I was embarrassed to admit I always showed up. Later, I realized that I thought that if I gave him what he needed or what I imagined he needed, he'd take better care of himself. I hated to see him suffer. I also thought he expected me to show up because I was his mother. During that time, he even said he knew I would never let him end up on the street. The truth is, Ryan never directly asked for my help.

My therapist suggested I visit a replica of the *Pietà* at the Saints Peter and Paul Church in San Francisco's North Beach. I had seen Michelangelo's statue of Mary holding the dead Christ when I was a young girl, during the 1964 World's Fair in New York. I was struck by how large Mary seemed in contrast with the body of Christ draped across her lap. It wasn't just her size; it was her presence, her courage to hold her lifeless, tortured son. I wanted to climb up on that lap and have her hold me, too.

On Christmas Eve, Ryan and I went to see the *Pietà*, and the size discrepancy upset him. While we knelt before her, Ryan said, "Look at her legs in comparison with Christ's. She's huge; he looks so puny."

As an artist, he was talking about the intent of the sculptor's design, but he was also responding to the power of the image. As we left, he said, "I didn't like seeing Christ looking so weak, so powerless."

Maybe I rushed in uninvited to rescue Ryan because I couldn't tolerate the thought of ending up like Mary, holding my dead son on my lap. During Christ's struggle to Calvary, Mary stood by him but did not interfere as he was whipped and jeered. I had a hard time allowing my son the dignity of his own fall.

* * *

During the two months Ryan lived with us, he steadily got stronger and eventually decided it was time to return to Los Angeles. He was eager to start life anew with Joyce. It seemed premature to me. He made plans to return in early February, but three days before his departure he came home from visiting his friend Ed and nonchalantly announced, "I lost my wallet."

He shrugged off my questions about flying without an ID or losing his medical insurance card and bus card, not to mention the money I had given him the day before. He seemed unconcerned. He had become accustomed to someone else picking up the pieces and things going awry.

That weekend, my friend Judith gave me a silver goddess medallion with the word FORGIVE imprinted on the back of it. She knew I was having a hard time forgiving myself for my son's mental illness and addiction. Coincidentally, I read a *New York Times* piece, "My Addicted Son," by David Sheff. It was about a father who kept showing up for his son, paying for successive rehabilitations, and offering him a warm, loving home with his second family, and still his son went out repeatedly and used. The author reflected in the article about whether he and his ex-wife, his son's mother, should have worked harder to maintain their marriage, should have lived somewhere else, could have done this or that to provide their son with a better safety net. I identified with him completely.

I tried to provide my son with a strong safety net, but a net cannot catch everything—the wallet slipped through one hole; his jobs slipped through another; his health, his sanity, slipped through others I could not mend. Still, I wove the net tighter each time another crisis occurred. I engaged in one rescue mission after another. I repeatedly cleaned up his messes. In therapy, I discovered I had not forgiven myself for his suffering. I also hadn't forgiven him for destroying the dreams I had for him. He was going to be the artist I had never become.

Before he left for Los Angeles, we went for an afternoon walk along the windy bay. We spent some time watching a construction crew framing a new houseboat along the waterfront.

Then Ryan asked a powerful question: "I've heard about your fear, I've heard about your waking up in the middle of the night in a sweat from a dream that something awful is happening to me, but I've never heard you talk about any positive dreams for me. Do you carry any positive images of my future?"

He was right. I hadn't had any positive images, and I certainly hadn't voiced any for a long time. I carried an image of him lying unconscious from an accidental overdose, paramedics working feverishly to revive him, or an image of him falling from the fire escape while trying to break into his own apartment. These images were rooted in history. I stumbled with my response. "I've always been your biggest fan. You know that."

He waited for more.

I tried again. "I can see you as a successful artist; I can see you as a teacher; I can see you having a successful relationship with your girlfriend—"

He interrupted, "I've already been all of those things, Mom. I've had success as an artist, I've been a good teacher, and I've had great girlfriends. I want to know what you see for me *now*."

I had nothing more to say. In that moment, I didn't see a normal future for my son. Years earlier, I had imagined him living with his girlfriend, selling his paintings, playing drums in various bands in San Francisco. But that had been in his late twenties and early thirties, when everything still seemed possible—before his illness had begun to rob him of his life. Now, at thirty-seven, he was asking me for my belief in his redemption.

He called Southwest Airlines to ask how he could get on the plane without a photo ID. He told them he had his birth certificate. I wondered how that would help. A baby's footprint wouldn't identify him now. But Southwest said they'd accept it.

He packed and got ready to leave. We went for a final walk down the pier, and I gave him the goddess medallion. He turned it over and saw the word FORGIVE.

"I want you to know I forgive myself for your mental illness, for your addiction, for your suffering," I said. "And I forgive you, too."

He sighed.

I continued, "I hope you can forgive yourself as well."

He looked at the figure of the goddess and traced the imprint of a spiral in her womb with his finger. "I'm glad you forgive me, Mom," he said, as he turned the medallion over in his hand. He looked at me. "That makes it easier for me to forgive myself."

Then he began to talk about all the losses in his life: his buddies who had stopped seeing him and no longer returned his calls; his girlfriends who had gone on to marry other men.

"I'm afraid to get too close to anyone now; I'm afraid I'll let them down."

I began to cry when he hugged me good-bye. "Mom, it's not as if I'm leaving for college," he joked. "There's no reason to cry."

My tears were for our history of what happened after our good-byes. It had been twenty years since I'd sent him off to college to meet his destiny. Since then, after each crisis, I had repeatedly swooped in to rescue him, with no lasting effect. Every time we said good-bye, I was fearful something terrible would happen to him again.

* * *

My anxiety over Ryan's uncertain future in Los Angeles continued. I sought support from a dual-diagnosis family group sponsored by NAMI and held at the local hospital. Room 19 held one large couch pushed against a wall, and we created a circle with an assortment of hard-backed plastic chairs. In regular attendance on Thursday nights were concerned mothers, sisters, stepmothers, and an occasional grandmother or aunt. Bill was usually the only man present. We found it curious that male family members stayed away. I wondered whether women felt more responsible for their loved ones' disabilities.

I was surprised at the range of afflictions as family members told their stories. Vivien, a regular with bright red hair, spoke about her fifty-three-year-old sister: "I keep wishing she would snap out of it and stop eating. She sleeps and eats all day, and now she weighs four hundred pounds. I don't care if she has an eating disorder; I can't stand how big she's gotten. When I was growing up in Lebanon, I used to think that every village had its idiot. Now it seems to me like more and more people are mentally ill."

What she said was cruel, but she was right. It did seem as if we were in the middle of a mental-illness epidemic.

Then Roberta spoke. "My forty-four-year-old daughter, who is a hoarder currently living in public housing, has never been adequately diagnosed. I don't know what she has, but she takes medication to control her hallucinations." Roberta had a quiet air of authority. She had long, silver-streaked brown hair and wore a gray wool cardigan. Like a den mother, she had a ready answer to almost anyone's questions, which had bugged me at first. But I did make a mental note to ask her how her daughter had gotten public housing.

Sitting next to her was Tina, a short, surprisingly cheerful woman who had two mentally ill adult children. Her son, twenty-six, suffered from schizoaffective disorder and had been in a locked psychiatric facility for six months. He couldn't wait to get out to use the medical marijuana card he'd received before his hospitalization from a psychiatrist who was now under investigation for licensing violations.

"The marijuana exacerbates his condition," Tina said. "At first when he smoked pot it relaxed him, but then he got totally out of control and started breaking things in the house. I had to call the police eleven times."

Carol, a psychiatric nurse and the mother of a bipolar, alcoholic, forty-year-old son who had been missing for a month, addressed all of us.

"I think each one of us is suffering from PTSD—post-traumatic stress disorder. We are trying to survive the trauma of having a family member with a mental illness. We are just as vulnerable to the unpredictability of the illness as our loved ones are."

True. I was a wreck. I was always on high alert, waiting for the next crisis. When the phone rang, I was sure someone was calling to tell me Ryan was dead. Everyone in our group looked shell-shocked and sleep-deprived from constant worry.

Ralph, a father in his mid-forties, who was attending for the first time, spoke next. "My son is a musician in his early twenties. He's never been diagnosed, but it's clear he has a mental illness. His pot smoking is out of control. I came here tonight because I want as much information as possible so I can catch it early."

I was struck by his term "catch it early"—as if finding the perfect treatment for his son's condition might eradicate it. Nevertheless, I empathized with his longing. I, too, wanted to find the right treatment, the cure, when Ryan first became ill. But by now most people in the group accepted that there was no way to nip mental illness and addiction in the bud.

Instead, we gathered to find ways to help one another cope with the roller coaster ride of a coexisting disorder. We discussed how to help our loved ones live with dignity without going broke ourselves. Many of us, including me, had a family member who did not qualify for governmental support (social security insurance (SSI) or disability benefits (SSDI), and we bore the burden of supporting them financially. Beyond financial worries, we faced other issues as well: guilt, broken marriages, stigmatization, and fear about the future.

Laura, a feisty Italian American woman in her mid-forties, started talking about her twenty-four-year old son, missing for weeks, who had just been found in a hospital in Los Angeles. She was grateful he was alive, relieved he was compliant with his medication, yet wary about bringing him home.

"I don't think my marriage is going to last with all of these crises. My husband, who is my son's stepfather, is sick and tired of my son's disappearing act. He's blown through thirty thousand dollars he received from a car accident settlement in the last month. My husband says we have no life outside of my son's dramas."

I spoke up. "Bill's thirty-seven-year-old daughter won't visit us because she doesn't agree with the way I support my son financially. Ryan's father's new wife doesn't *believe* in mental illness and won't allow Ryan in their home. She doesn't want his behavior to affect their son. The stigmatization of mental illness isn't limited to the patient."

Others sighed in agreement. At the end of the meeting, Laura came up to me. "I don't want to be in these rooms in seventeen years, like you, still struggling with these issues, wondering where my kid is and if he's using."

I didn't blame her; I didn't want to be there, either. I found it difficult to sit in that room, listening to each person detail the deterioration of a loved one's life. Initially, it was comforting to know I wasn't alone, but after about ten months of meetings, they became too depressing for me to continue.

As we drove home that night, Bill said, "Tonight, every family member was talking about the need to keep their loved one *safe*."

Yes, safety *was* the prevailing theme of the meeting. And I wondered whether it would help if more fathers participated in their child's treatment. Specifically, could Ryan's condition improve if Jerry accepted the complexity of his illness, instead of belittling his failure to get his life together? Were the fathers absent because they were trying to keep themselves safe from having to face the devastation of their child's illness?

chapter 12

the second letter

In May, Ryan left a familiar message on my cell phone.

"Mom, it's over between Joyce and me. Last night she threw me out and I spent the night on the street. I have no place to go. Call me."

When Ryan had returned to Los Angeles in February, I had already been concerned it wouldn't last. I sensed that Joyce had fallen in love with Ryan the artist, whose work she admired, not the man with a serious disability. I was grateful she had been steadfast during his hospitalization with endocarditis and offered great emotional support during his recuperation. But it had become clear that she wanted a self-supporting partner who didn't have to rely on his parents for housing or food. In fact, Ryan had just been denied Social Security disability and Medicare benefits. He couldn't even pay his bills.

When I returned his call, he sounded panicked about not having a place to stay and vague about why he and Joyce had broken up. "It's just not working out. I'd like to come back to Northern California. I've talked to Michael about staying with him in San Francisco until I can find a job and a place of my own."

Michael was the friend who had offered him a place to stay the year before. I knew they had worked together in the '90s at a computer start-up company. Michael had been very ill with an HIV-related illness but had regained his strength enough to work part-time.

"Does Michael have room for you in his apartment?"

"He has a one-bedroom but says I can stay on his couch. While he's at work, I can use his computer to get my skills up to speed so I can apply for a job at the agency where he's working."

"That's very generous. In the meantime, how are you going to support yourself?" Ryan was on a very low budget, which Jerry and I were providing.

"Michael said we can split expenses and he can help me with my SSDI appeal. I should get back pay from when I was first diagnosed with endocarditis, and then I can pay him back."

The letter he had received from the Social Security Administration stated he was "not disabled enough" to receive disability insurance. The decision to deny was based on his treatment history and answers he had given on his application form in November. The denial stated, "Although you do have discomfort, the medical evidence shows you are still able to move about and to use your arms, hands, and legs in a satisfactory manner. You are able to occasionally lift fifty pounds and frequently lift twenty-five pounds, stand and walk up to six hours in a normal eight-hour workday. . . . Though you may be depressed at times, your records show you are able to think, communicate, and act in your own interest."

What did the ability to lift a fifty-pound weight have to do with a brain disorder and a weakened heart valve? I was furious.

While he was still in the hospital, Ryan asked the psychiatrist who had treated him for six months to fill out the necessary diagnostic paperwork. She agreed, but she never responded to his subsequent letter, his repeated phone calls, or my phone calls or e-mails to her clinical assistant. "I'll make sure she gets the message," her assistant assured me. Because there was no response from his primary treating psychiatrist, the Social Security Administration required him to have an evaluation by one of its own contract psychiatrists. That evaluation would be the deciding factor in determining whether he was impaired enough to receive benefits.

Shortly after he moved in with Joyce, he took three buses to the designated Social Security Administration office in Los Angeles, where he was handed a blank copy of the same sixteen-page application he had filled out months before. He was then told to fill it out again. Wisely, he had brought a copy of his original, including his treatment history. After filling it out and waiting two hours, he was called into the psychiatrist's office. He told me the doctor didn't bother to look at him while he perused the paperwork. Looking down at the form, he asked Ryan:

"Name?"

"Ryan."

"Birth date?"

"December 12, 1967."

"Age?"

"Thirty-seven."

"Occupation?"

"Advertising art director."

"I see you were born in the Philippines."

At that point, Ryan asked the psychiatrist to look at him. Ryan is short, slim, light-complexioned, and dark-haired. He looks decidedly Irish American.

"Doctor, do I look like I was born in the Philippines? I was born in Philadelphia, not the Philippines. See, right there, it says Philadelphia."

The psychiatrist glanced up at him for a second. Looking down again, he continued, "Oh, yes, Philadelphia. Well, I'm from Boston. The Philippines, Philadelphia—it's all the same to me."

When the psychiatrist finished reviewing the paperwork, he said, "Good luck" and dismissed Ryan without looking up at him, again.

Ryan called me when he left the building. "Mom, I'm definitely not going to get SSDI. The only way I could have gotten it would have been if I'd had peanut butter coming out of my ears. You should have seen the other people in the waiting room. They were all ranting and raving about suing the Department of Water and Power because they're sure their water is poisoned. I'm just not delusional enough."

His joke made me laugh and took the edge off what must have been a humiliating experience for him. The truth behind his humor was grim. Whether or not the interview with the psychiatrist had happened the way Ryan relayed it, I believed him. The way the system works, a person has to be actively delusional or a very good actor to be considered disabled enough to receive support. Ryan was not going to exaggerate a condition that caused him shame. Why would anyone who was always at the top of his class in school, had a graduate degree, and had held responsible jobs in advertising have tried to convince someone he was mentally ill?

Ryan moved in with Michael, who made good on his promise to help Ryan practice his computer skills, but he still didn't have any luck finding a job. Two months later, he did find a studio apartment in the heart of downtown San Francisco. In July, Bill and I helped him move in. Liz found a desk and a table on the curb outside her house; we added pots and pans and kitchen utensils, as well as a blow-up bed, until he could get a futon.

The next day I drove the six hours to Los Angeles to teach my summer course at UCLA. I planned to bring back Ryan's computer, printer, and art supplies, which were housed in storage. Before I left, I found an attorney who agreed to help Ryan with his SSDI appeal. Things were starting to fall into place.

When I returned several weeks later, amid the pile of mail that had accumulated was a letter from Joyce. I didn't want to open it. Would this be a repeat of the other damaging letter I had received from Ryan's previous girlfriend Holly describing his drug use? Jerry told me he had also received a letter from Joyce describing the incident that ended their relationship. I waited a day before opening the letter and then asked Bill to read it first.

"It's going to be difficult for you to read, but it's nothing you haven't heard before," he said.

Indeed, it was Joyce's graphic description of the incident that shook me. The night she threw him out, Joyce found Ryan naked, with his belt pulled tight around his arm, shooting up in the bathroom of their apartment. Blood was splattered all over his arms, bloodstained tissues crumpled around him. After she took away his syringe and drug kit, she told him to leave.

Ryan was injecting drugs even though he had almost died

eight months before from the bacterial infection in his heart caused by IV drug use. At the time, Dr. Murphy had told him, in front of the whole family, that he would die if he ever injected himself again. I still wanted to believe his main problem was his bipolar illness, which I thought was manageable, but my belief had blinded me to what I didn't want to see. I was devastated.

Several nights before I received the letter, I had a dream that scared me awake. In the dream, Lieutenant Van Buren, a character on the television series *Law & Order*, handed me a heavy cardboard box that contained an open plastic bag filled with the cremated remains of my son and me. Our ashes were commingled, our bones pulverized by the heat of the flames. Van Buren gave me a look of no-nonsense compassion. I couldn't get back to sleep that night. It was true: his illness was killing us both.

The writings of one of my UCLA students paralleled my dream. Beth wrote a piece about her brother's recent death. A drug user, he too had been hospitalized with endocarditis; his damaged heart valve had been replaced, and yet he had died some months later in his sleep. "One morning he just didn't wake up," she wrote. She felt conflicted about his death because they had been estranged. She described him as "the prodigal son." Their mother had always taken him in, no matter how many times he had borrowed money or had scrapes with the law. Beth had been "the good daughter," doing everything right, and she resented her brother's claim on their mother's love. Beth's brother's disregard for his life and her mother's continuing support of his profligacy hit too close to home. I knew that Liz, too, resented the expenditures of both my attention and my money on her brother. I tried to make it up to her, but there was little I could do to heal her own grief about her brother's illness or to remove the burden she felt being the "normal one."

I called Ryan and told him that I had received a letter from Joyce and we needed to talk in person. I went to his apartment. I sat on the floor, because there was nowhere else to sit except the inflatable bed I had lent him. The components of his computer and cables I had brought back from Los Angeles were spread out all over the hardwood floor. Ryan lay back on the inflated bed. I asked him to sit up as I read Joyce's letter out loud. He had his own copy, which Joyce had sent him, on his lap. I read it out loud anyway. I wanted us both to hear Joyce's words. Near the end of the letter, I choked back tears, not so much from the horrific scene she described but because she had loved him, believed in him and his resolve to stay clean. In spite of his betrayal, she still cared enough to write the letter.

Ryan denied nothing. I told him he had to go into addiction treatment or I would cut off all financial support. "You're sick," I said emphatically. "You have a serious drug problem, and you can't get well on your own. You've been dealing with this for seventeen years." I then read from a list I had written of incidents that had occurred in the past two years that had jeopardized his health, destroyed his relationships, resulted in job losses, and threatened him with jail time. "What do you want to do about it?" I asked.

"I do have a problem," he said flatly, sitting forward without looking at me. It was the first time he had said those words, but his tone lacked resolve and any genuine acknowledgment of the depth of his problem. He didn't say, "I know I have a problem. I need help. I know I've hurt other people." No, his statement sounded as if he had rehearsed the words he thought I wanted to hear.

I waited for him to say more. When he didn't, I wearily recited the names of a couple of local treatment programs for him to contact. He looked for a piece of paper on his bed to write them down. Before thinking, I offered him a piece of paper from my yellow pad. I was always offering him something: health insurance, an apartment, therapy, new sneakers. That was my problem.

chapter 13

reducing harm isn't easy

The following week, Ryan started to attend weekly therapy sessions at the Center for Harm Reduction Therapy (CHRT) in San Francisco. CHRT treats drug users with the philosophy of reducing drug-related harm by helping them decrease their substance use as they move toward abstinence. Harm reduction requires that the drug user and the treatment provider work together to identify the triggers for use and plan strategies to avoid those triggers. At the same time, I joined a CHRT-sponsored family group whose focus was to help family members reduce the harm we did to ourselves by learning how to deal constructively with a family member who had an addiction.

Several weeks after joining the group, I agreed to meet Ryan at his apartment to take care of some of his immediate financial needs: a bus pass, a check for probation from his former cocaine-possession charge in Los Angeles, and a therapy check. We soon strayed into territory I had not agreed upon.

I picked up Ryan, and we drove to city hall to buy his bus pass. Afterward, we sat in the car as I wrote out the checks for probation and therapy. One of the conditions of my continued financial support was that he attend weekly therapy sessions. When I started to write the probation check for the owed amount of $200, Ryan said, "Write the check for one hundred and fifty dollars, and I'll use the other fifty dollars in cash to get my iPod out of the pawnshop."

"What do you mean? You told me probation was two hundred dollars, and we never discussed your iPod being in a pawnshop. Don't you have to pay your probation installment in full by the end of this year? What's your iPod doing in a pawnshop?"

He sulked and said, "Write the check for two hundred dollars, then."

I wrote the probation check and found myself reacting to his sulking, instead of finding out why he had pawned his iPod. I couldn't stand the deep freeze, the disconnection. Ryan didn't usually employ the silent treatment with me; that had been a dreaded tactic of my mother's after she had been drinking. I felt shut out, just as I had felt as a child with my mother. Without thinking, I asked if he wanted to go to the pawnshop and see if they'd take my credit card to get his iPod out.

Before long, we parked in a loading zone in front of Mission Jewelry & Loan and Ryan got out of the car. "Stay here," he said. "I don't want you to go in there. I'm embarrassed."

He walked like an old man in his oversize black jacket, limping from whatever sore on his leg he didn't want me to see. He came back to say they would accept a debit card only. We parked, went in, and took our place in the cashier's line. We were surrounded by cases of gold jewelry and an assortment of guitars and horns hanging from the ceiling.

I felt sickened that my son's life and mine had sunk to this level. I suspected, without needing Ryan to admit it, that he had pawned his iPod for drugs. It took a long time for the cashier to locate Ryan's iPod, but he finally deducted $60 from my debit card and we hurried out. The whole experience left me disgusted both with Ryan and with myself.

At the next CHRT family group, which took place in a small office in Oakland, I described my pawnshop fiasco. There were six of us that night: three mothers of addicts, one sister of an alcoholic, the husband of an alcoholic, and Patt, our facilitator. Patt was a sturdy woman in her early fifties with an open, youthful face and short white hair. She dressed comfortably in slacks and a loose short-sleeved shirt, often with a Hawaiian motif, no matter what the weather. It was a hot night, and the hum from the air conditioner in the window competed with the tones of the gospel choir rehearsing in the Baptist church next door.

I revealed my inability to hold the limit I had set for myself with Ryan. Patt, who had the patience and wisdom of Solomon, responded, "Now you know what it feels like for a person with drug problems to relapse. One part of you is saying, *No, I'm never going to use again*, while at the same time another part is on the phone, calling your dealer and making arrangements for a buy. It's like there are two separate parts of you operating simultaneously. Neither one knows what the other one is doing. Just imagine how you'd feel when you found yourself using."

"I know," I said, nodding in agreement. "That's exactly how I felt—out of control and totally disgusted with myself. I didn't even know who was behind the wheel of the car as I drove to the pawnshop. I was prepared to pay for the bus pass, prepared for the therapy check, prepared for the probation check. That was my agreement and the limit I had set for myself. But when Ryan withdrew and gave me the cold shoulder, all of a sudden I put the car in gear and backed up. My bottom line went right out the window. I was just as dependent on my connection with him as if I had been caught in the grip of a drug."

After listening to my disappointment in myself, Martha, a woman in her early fifties, turned to me and said, "What if you had no hope?"

"No hope?" I asked, unsure whether I had heard her correctly.

"Yes. What if you had no hope?"

"What do you mean, no hope? I *need* hope. I've been through periods of having no hope, when Ryan was in the hospital with endocarditis and I thought he was going to die. I got incredibly depressed. I don't want to go through that again."

"No," she said. "That sounds like hopelessness, which is different from no hope. That sounds like you were in despair."

I nodded. "Yes, I was in despair."

"Having no hope means that you no longer harbor hope that things will change, that things will be different. Instead, you stay with what is."

"You mean I'll get to a point where I'll accept that this is the way it is? I don't think I could stand that."

"No, I don't think you ever accept that this is the way it is," interrupted Patt, "but you acknowledge that this is the way it is right now, instead of holding out hope that things will be different—if he gets clean, if he engages in therapy, if such-and-such happens. We know all of that is magical thinking. Instead, you stay in the present. This is the way it is right now, instead of this is the way it's going to be, or this is the way it could be, or this is the way I want it to be."

This was a very different approach to looking at Ryan's addiction and mental illness. If I accepted this new way of thinking, I would have to acknowledge and accept the reality of Ryan's problems in all their horror. Instead of focusing on what I *should* do or *could* do, to help him, I would be forced to deal with my own feelings—as painful as those would be.

* * *

When I told my therapist, Mike, about the pawnshop incident, he suggested I visit the *Pietà* again. On a brisk December day, I entered the cathedral and knelt before the magnificent statue of Mary holding her dead son. She held his sprawled body on her lap with her right hand, yet her left hand was open in a gesture of surrender. She did not show anguish. Her serene face reflected her acceptance of the inevitable. She could not save her thirty-three-year-old son, no matter that he was a mystic, a prophet, and, some thought, mad. It was his destiny to die.

Hold and surrender. Hold and let go. What a teaching the *Pietà* embodies for us mothers. We can hold and support our children in a deeply personal way for a limited time only, but ultimately, for their own good and ours, we have to let them go. I had tried to keep my son safe by providing for him. In retrospect, my continued involvement in his life may have done him more harm than good. My endless rescue missions allowed him to avoid working on himself and prevented him from finding his own resources. I may have needed him in my life more than he wanted or needed me. These were very hard lessons to learn, because I kept repeating them.

I knelt before Mary and asked for the courage to accept what is. To accept a son who was very ill, did not fit within society's norms, and yet had to find a way to survive. I couldn't change him, and I couldn't change the world around him. I was beginning to understand the concept of letting go. At the same time, I had not yet embraced actual surrender.

chapter 14

mothers don't let go

Ryan spent his thirty-eighth birthday in San Francisco's county jail. The family was all set to celebrate his birthday with an Italian dinner in North Beach. His gifts were wrapped. My granddaughters, his nieces, had made him a cardboard crown festooned with plastic jewels. Instead, Ryan was decked out in an orange jumpsuit and wrist bracelets, held in restraints in a "safe cell" downtown. His crime: At midnight on the previous, cold December night, he had thrown a flowerpot through the plate-glass door of his apartment building because he had forgotten his key and none of the other tenants had responded to his ringing their buzzers for entry. The building manager called the police, and the next day he called and berated me.

"You knew your son had a drug problem when you cosigned the lease. You didn't want him in your house, so you dumped him on us."

"You don't know what you're talking about," I said, and he backed off. But what he said was a truth I wouldn't admit.

Instead, I told him I'd come in from Sausalito to look at the damage. First, however, Bill and I drove to the police station at 850 Bryant Street to find Ryan. We waited in line while a young police officer eventually checked for Ryan's name on the computer. He'd been transferred to the psych ward at San Francisco General Hospital on a seventy-two-hour hold. He would be released after he was arraigned, within the next day or two. Before I even asked, the officer said, "No, ma'am, you cannot visit him."

We went to Ryan's apartment building to survey and photograph the damage. Because I had cosigned the lease, Bill was concerned I'd be liable. One of the glass panels on the front door was shattered. When the building manager let me into Ryan's studio apartment, I saw two syringes lying on the floor.

The building manager cynically asked me if Ryan was diabetic. I shook my head, no. His hospital toxicology report was negative for drugs, but his apartment told another story.

Bill and I spent the next two days packing up the apartment and putting Ryan's belongings in storage. The felony vandalism charge was dropped to a misdemeanor because of my assurance to the landlord that we would pay for damage and move Ryan out of the building. At the sentencing hearing, the judge dismissed the charges and told Ryan to get out of his courtroom and stay out.

I was left to ponder my intervention—a mixture of panic, embarrassment, and shame. In some ways, I was more appalled by the state of his apartment than I was by his vandalism. There were unwashed dishes, glasses, and pans piled high in his sink, fruit flies feeding on the refuse in overflowing garbage bags on the floor, bloodstains on the side of the bathtub, and bills strewn everywhere. I could accept that throwing a flowerpot through the glass door was an act by a mentally ill person. However, his living in squalor, I naively thought, implied that I had not taught Ryan responsibility. Of course, his lack of housekeeping had nothing to do with me.

Yet I agreed completely with David Sheff when he wrote, "We are connected to our children no matter what. They are interwoven into each cell and inseparable from every neuron. They supersede our consciousness, swell in our every hollow and cavity and recess with our most primitive instincts, deeper even than our identities, deeper even than ourselves."

I started to clean. I tried to atone for my shame by doing countless loads of laundry. I washed, dried, folded, and packed them into boxes that I labeled "lights" and "darks." I cleaned compulsively to bring order to the chaos of my son's life and to mine.

When I called my daughter, Liz, to say that things with Ryan seemed to be getting worse, she disagreed. "It's always been this way," she said, "as long as he's been bipolar."

"This bad for the past seventeen years?" I asked.

"If that's how long it's been since he was diagnosed, then yes. He has no judgment and no morals. And *you* have a bad memory."

I empathized with Liz, but her comments about my relationship with Ryan always stung, and I was not going to abandon him.

It was hard to admit that Ryan was no longer the golden child/ artist I had championed. He was a man with an illness that caused him to do the most self-serving and expedient thing in front of him, regardless of the cost to others. He may not have set out to hurt others deliberately, but he didn't seem to notice when he did.

135

* * *

Ryan spent the remainder of December surfing the couches of friends and relatives. Then the new year found him "officially homeless." One night in early January, Ryan stayed with Bill and me on the houseboat. We were about to move to an apartment in the city, so packing boxes were everywhere. Ryan slept in the loft.

The next morning, I found him snoring on the floor, huddled in a fetal position next to the air mattress. At first I was surprised by the sight of his bare legs. His ankles and calves looked swollen, and there was blood on the back of his right calf. I was alarmed, thinking about the abscesses he had developed when he had endocarditis. I went downstairs to get Bill. When he saw Ryan's leg, he said, "Cover him up; he must be cold."

As I put the blanket over him, I noticed a dirty spoon on a packing box next to his body. I picked up the spoon, thinking Ryan must have made some hot chocolate before he went to sleep. Upon further inspection, I saw that the outer rim of the spoon was charred. His lighter was on the floor next to him. Without thinking, I put the tip of my tongue to the spoon and tasted the bitterness. That wasn't chocolate congealed on the spoon; it was heroin. I rolled my son over and found a syringe with half a barrel of brown gunk lying underneath his body. He stirred.

I started yelling, "How could you do this here, in my house? How could you do this to me and to Bill after all we've tried to do to help you? How could you do this to yourself?"

"What are you talking about? I didn't do anything," he mumbled as he barely looked at me.

I picked up the syringe and the dirty spoon and practically shoved them into his face.

"Look at this," I hissed. "This isn't nothing."

He looked away.

"I didn't do anything," he said.

"I want to know what this is," I yelled, pointing to the residue on the spoon. "I just put it to my tongue, and I want to know what crap I've tasted."

He didn't answer. He could barely keep his eyes open.

"Get up," I said. "Come downstairs. Clean the blood off your legs. We're getting out of here."

I didn't know where I was going to take him. It was all I could do to restrain myself from hitting him. He had repeatedly sworn—to me and his therapist—that he hadn't used drugs in the last six months. And why, until now, had I believed he would not use drugs in my home?

My friend Lonny, an ER doctor who was an expert on addiction, had told me I was fooling myself when I said Ryan wasn't using. "He's an addict. Addicts use," Lonny said. "And they aren't selective about where they use." I felt like a fool.

Bill and I tried to figure out our options. Call the police. Drive him to rehab. Dump him on the street. My hands shook as I made coffee. We were due to meet the painters at our new apartment within the next hour; then I had to get to work. We decided to take two cars to the apartment; after we met the painters, I would take Ryan to the nearest rehab center, in the Mission.

For the first time, I gave Ryan an ultimatum: "You go into rehab today or I never want to see you again. I mean it. You're destroying yourself, you're destroying me, you're destroying the whole family."

I felt betrayed and hopeless. While I cried, Ryan sat at the breakfast table and said, "I would give you a hug, Mom, but I don't think you want me anywhere near you."

"That's right," I said.

We left the houseboat, got into the car, and, still high, Ryan nodded off as I drove over the Golden Gate Bridge. At the new apartment, while Bill and I talked with the painters, Ryan sat on the floor of one of the empty, unpainted rooms, fumbling on his cell phone with the rehab numbers I had provided.

I drove Ryan to the Resource Center, a social services referral agency for drug treatment in the Mission district. On the curb outside the center, a number of forlorn-looking men and women loitered. That area of the city was known as "heroin central."

Ryan disappeared through the front door of the building, and I drove off. When I updated Lonny on Ryan's situation, he said, "I hate to be cynical, but you just chauffeured him to his dealer."

* * *

Ryan spent February trying to get into one of the limited number of residential drug treatment programs that accepted addicts with a dual diagnosis. While he waited for a placement, Liz allowed him to camp out for a month in the backyard playhouse her husband and Bill were building for her girls. There was no heat or electricity, but at least he had shelter from the rain and the cold. Ryan found regular homeless shelters too noisy.

"There are too many men snoring," he said. "I can't get any sleep."

Bill made it clear that Ryan could not stay with us while he waited for admittance into rehab—he felt betrayed by Ryan's heroin use in our home. I agreed, but we periodically allowed him into the apartment to shower or have a hot meal. He usually arrived wearing three jackets: a gray outer wind-and-rain shell, a black jacket, and a thin blue Giants baseball jacket that served as insulation. My heart broke every time I saw him.

One visit in mid-February, he told me about having spent several hours the previous day in the ER at San Francisco General after a pickup truck speeding through an intersection had allegedly hit him on his bike. He claimed that if he hadn't been wearing a helmet, he would be dead. He had stitches near his right temple, and his hand was swollen to the size of a catcher's mitt from breaking his fall. I took his hand in mine and looked at the swelling.

"Did they x-ray your hand? It looks broken."

"It's not broken, Mom. I know how to fall from so many years of skateboarding. But my helmet is completely shattered. December and January were bad months, Mom, but things are turning around."

I noticed that he was wearing a filigreed silver cross on a chain around his neck. When I asked him about it, he said that ever since he had seen a show of the Assisi frescoes a few years before, Jesus had been his main man. This was news to me. I knew he stopped into churches from time to time for some peace and quiet, but I did not know of his allegiance to Jesus.

I was raised Catholic, and my children were baptized, but Jerry and I did not raise them in the Church. I left the Church when my parish priest told me I could no longer receive the sacraments because of my use of contraception after our children were born. I attended Mass sporadically and found some solace in prayer and meditation but questioned the existence of a God.

Maybe it was a mistake not to give my children a foundation to push against. Maybe Ryan was looking for something to fill the void in his soul. He asked if he could shave and take a shower, wash his jeans and jackets. He wanted to get the bloodstains out of his jeans. He said he hadn't eaten in three days, and when he removed his T-shirt to wash it, his ribs protruded and his chest looked like a nine-year-old's. I tried to quiet my anxiety and grief by taking deep breaths and sticking to simple tasks: heat up soup, pour him some apple juice, get a towel from the linen closet for his bath.

After he took a bath, we sat at the breakfast table and he told me about the possibility of a studio apartment in Oakland if a bed at a treatment facility didn't open up soon.

"They evicted some guy from this apartment in Oakland, and the manager said they need time to fix up the place. She liked me, so she might rent it to me on a month-to-month basis. I just have to get a copy of my disability check to her to show I have reliable income."

We had hired a lawyer to help Ryan appeal the denial of his Social Security disability benefits for a heart condition, and he had just received a letter stating he had won the appeal. He would soon receive $859 per month in disability insurance. I doubted it would cover his rent and living expenses, but it might enable him at least to get housing. The caseworker at the Resource Center had put him on a list for public housing but had told him it would take months to years before anything opened up.

All of a sudden, Ryan started talking rapidly about his bike accident. "I was biking along Twenty-Third Street and saw the pickup truck careening down the hill. He was going about fifty miles per hour."

"I didn't know you had a bike," I said.

"Yeah, Liz lent me one she found on the street. It's old, but it's an okay ride. When the truck hit me, I flew about thirty feet in the air. I don't think the driver saw me, but the kids who witnessed it said he accelerated after impact. They couldn't get his license plate numbers he sped away so fast. So he must have known he hit something."

His story was fantastical, and I could barely keep up with his delivery.

"One good thing came out of this, Mom. When I went to the emergency room and told them that I had endocarditis last year, they did a full chest X-ray and complete blood panel. I'm clear. I just have to monitor my temperature and take antibiotics four times a day because of the incision in my head. You know, to be safe."

To be safe? *He isn't safe. There is nothing safe about him*, I thought. When Ryan was a boy, he bounced back easily from skateboarding falls and bone breaks. That was then. Now that he was thirty-eight, his quick recoveries were behind him. I looked at the scars on his body and wondered how much more abuse he could sustain, and how much more I could endure.

* * *

That night I dreamed that my best friend, Connie, said, "Don't forget the unknown part of the God story about your son. There are parts of the God story, his soul's journey, you know nothing about. Can know nothing about."

A week later, I received a call from the ER at San Francisco General, notifying me that a car making an illegal U-turn had plowed into Ryan, bruising his hip, spraining his ribs, and totaling his bike. The driver told the police she hadn't seen him. When Bill and I arrived at the ER and asked where we could find Ryan, the male nurse said with a smile, "Oh, yeah, the skateboarder. He was in here last week. He's probably outside, having a smoke."

We eventually found Ryan lying on a gurney in the hallway. He said he'd already had his chest x-rayed and was waiting for his discharge papers. A young, harried attending nurse let me know how uncooperative Ryan had been.

"He's been in and out of the ER holding area. He has to have his chest x-rayed, and we don't have time to be looking for him."

She scolded me as if it were my fault.

"I already had my chest x-rayed," Ryan said.

"There's no record of any chest x-ray in your chart," she said, as she stormed off.

Ryan shook his head. "They probably lost it." He eased himself off the gurney and limped outside for a cigarette. The nurse returned five minutes later with his chart.

"Where is he now? They're waiting for him in x-ray."

"I'll go outside and find him. He went outside for a smoke."

"Don't come back into the ER when you do," she said to me. "You're not supposed to be in here."

The area was filled with other waiting family members. They must have been with the good, cooperative patients. It was all I could do to hold my tongue. At the NAMI meetings, I heard stories about the rude treatment mothers of mentally ill or addicted children received from health care professionals.

Bill and I stayed in the waiting room while Ryan was x-rayed again. The waiting rooms of the ERs I had occupied over the years began to merge. We were a wide-eyed, ragtag tribe waiting for someone to tell us something, anything.

chapter 15

a constellation of crises

Two weeks later, I received a call from another hospital. The paramedics found Ryan at dawn, shoeless in the rain, staggering in the middle of the street. Dr. Lee, the psychiatrist on call at University of California San Francisco Medical Center, asked me to come quickly.

When I arrived, Ryan was in four-point restraints with tubes coming out of his arms and legs. Because of his recent traumas and accidents, I feared he was having a manic episode. He made guttural animal sounds and yelled and screamed. When I put my hand on his chest to try to calm him, my presence only riled him more. He screamed, "Fuck you. Get out of here."

Then he yelled, "Ma, Ma," over and over.

I broke down, and the nurses ushered me into a "quiet room."

Ryan's toxicology screen showed a mixture of heroin and cocaine in his system. Twenty-four hours later, the drugs had still not cleared out, and Dr. Lee called me to ask what else Ryan might have injected.

"I have no idea," I replied.

"We think whatever he took might have been laced with PCP, which often causes hallucinations."

Dr. Lee said he would hold Ryan for observation as long as possible. I pleaded with him to transfer Ryan to the psych ward at Langley Porter, where he would get care for his bipolar disorder. I also asked that he recommend substance abuse treatment. However, Dr. Lee maintained the necessity for medical monitoring in the hospital for the next twenty-four hours.

The following morning, when I arrived at Ryan's room on the fourteenth floor, I was notified that a hospital "sitter" had been assigned to prevent him from hurting himself. At daybreak, he asked her to open the window because he wanted to fly out with the birds. Despite his agitation, his silver cross still hung from the chain around his neck. He was disoriented, and his speech was slurred, but he recognized me.

"Hey, Mom, what's happening?" he said, as if nothing was wrong.

The nurse let me remove the restraint on his right wrist just long enough for me to feed him a sandwich and some juice. After that, he went to sleep and I left for work, relieved he was getting the care he needed.

At eight o'clock the next morning, I called and was encouraged to learn he was being transferred to the psychiatric hospital next door. But Dr. Lee called me at noon with contradictory news.

"Your son is much calmer today. He's not manic anymore. He's clear. We can't keep him in the hospital any longer. We have no legal right to hold him. I know you're going to be disappointed about this, but there's nothing more I can do. All I can do is give him a list of residential rehabs. He says he has a plan for after discharge."

"What do you mean, discharge?" I said. "He can't be discharged; he has no place to go. He's homeless. You saw him yesterday. He wanted to fly out the fourteenth-floor window."

"I know, but he's clear now. He told us there's an old hotel in Oakland where he can get a room. He says he's stayed there before."

"Yes, he stayed there once before, but that hotel is boarded up and marked for demolition. He can't stay there. He has no place to go, Dr. Lee."

I had learned that a homeless mentally ill patient could receive a discharge from a hospital if he said he had a favorite overpass under which to sleep or could name his favorite alley. Such options were considered "home" for a discharge. It hadn't always been this way. When I worked in mental health in the '70s, treatment for mentally ill people was inadequate, but at least they were housed and fed in institutions. Advocates for the mentally ill considered these institutions warehouses, and many were, but at least patients were not subjected to the violence and drug use that happened on the streets.

When I told Bill the news, he shook his head. "All Ryan had to do was say yes, and Dr. Lee would have found him a bed in a treatment facility."

Unfortunately, Ryan had the right to destroy his life. As my friend Connie said in the dream, I had no idea what his soul's journey entailed.

* * *

After his discharge, Ryan spent several weeks on and off the street. It was a particularly wet rainy season in the Bay Area, and he got worn down standing in lines at soup kitchens and trying to find shelter. He pursued residential treatment through his caseworker, Lauren, at the Resource Center. In April, she applied on his behalf to Baker Places, a dual-diagnosis residential treatment facility in San Francisco. In early May, Lauren told him he had been turned down for admission and the reasons weren't clear. She did know he had not received a "good referral." I was astounded that now that Ryan was finally asking for treatment, he couldn't get it. What would have been a convincing referral for a bipolar drug addict seeking help?

Ryan was disappointed about the rejection but stayed positive and decided to apply to Ohlhoff House, a sober-living facility. Although Ohlhoff House did not specifically treat patients with a dual diagnosis, it did accept people with both a substance abuse problem and a mental disorder such as a learning disability. I took Ryan to his intake assessment at a beautiful Edwardian mansion at the crest of a hill on Fell Street. I waited in the large living room, which doubled as a meeting room, while Ryan's intake took place. The intake director, Hector, told him that most of the men in the program had part- or full-time day jobs, attended nightly meetings, took their meals together, and slept in the house. Ryan would have to wait two to six weeks for an available bed, but Hector encouraged him to come to the Monday- and Thursday-night meetings to get to know the other men in the program.

Ryan and Hector shared a smoke on the porch before they shook hands and said good-bye. Ryan was very excited about the prospect of entering Ohlhoff House. "I really liked Hector," he said. "I let him know what medications I'm on, and he said they're all okay, but they don't have a psychiatrist on staff, so I'd still have to see my own psychiatrist. He told me to get my medical history in right away. I'd like to get my records at the Resource Center and fax them today."

"What's the hurry?" I asked.

"I want to impress him," he said, smiling.

It was good to see him smile. I drove him to the Resource Center, and he faxed his records in that day.

During the latter part of May and the first two weeks of June, Ryan went to every Monday- and Thursday-evening meeting. He was hopeful he'd be accepted. In the interim, I paid for his rooms at various cheap hotels and hostels in the North Beach area, away from his self-proclaimed "hot zone" of drugs in the Mission. His stay at each hotel seemed to end by the last day of the first week. There was always a reason—rooms were already reserved for the following week, the manager didn't like him, someone broke into his room in the middle of the night, another guest stole money out of his wallet. At the time, I thought it was odd and I was wary, but I actually believed some of his stories.

By the fifth week, when he ran out of options, Bill and I agreed to let him stay with us. The wet winter wore away our resolve not to rescue him. The first two nights went smoothly— he ate dinner with us, kept his unofficial curfew, and was fairly quiet. But on the third night, he was up at 2:00 A.M., banging into the wall in the hallway and dropping things into the bathroom sink. The fourth night, Bill found him in the guest room, dressed in his jacket and shirt but missing his pants and shoes. When Bill asked him what he was doing, he said, "I must have been sleepwalking."

After he left the following morning, we found a syringe on the hallway floor and another one wrapped up in a wad of toilet paper on the dresser. I almost stuck myself with the needle when I unwrapped the wad. The barrels of both syringes held remnants of heroin. I gagged.

When I called Lonny, he said, "His use and his desire to get clean are not contradictory. He's doing what drug users do. They use. That doesn't mean he doesn't want treatment. You can't know what's going on inside his head."

Ryan rang the bell at 10:00 P.M., expecting to reenter our apartment as if nothing had happened. Bill had already put all of Ryan's belongings in a black trash bag and met him at the front door.

"You can't stay here anymore. You used in our house. Get the hell out." Bill's voice was shaking. I had never seen him so angry. I stopped him from throwing the trash bag out into the street. It was too late for Ryan to go to a shelter—they all had curfews. Ryan wandered off up the street. I didn't sleep at all that night.

At seven the next morning, Ryan rang our doorbell and stood at the door with blood oozing from bruises and scrapes on his forehead and cheek. He could barely stand up or keep his eyes open; his knees started to buckle.

"What happened?" I asked. "Did you get beaten up?"

"No," he said, as he sat down wearily on the bottom step of our staircase. "I fell down the steps at the park."

Without challenging him, I asked, "Where's your black bag?" referring to the gym bag he'd had the previous night, which contained all of his meds, his cell phone, and his personal items.

"I couldn't carry it," he said. "It's too heavy. I left it at the park. I needed to clean up."

"There's a bathroom in the park," said Bill. "Use that."

"Let him clean up," I insisted, "and we'll drive him to the park to find his black bag."

While Ryan took a shower, Bill and I discussed what to do next. I had to start seeing my therapy clients at eight thirty. We decided to take him back to the Resource Center. Four months earlier, I had told him I wouldn't see him again unless he got into treatment. I had not held him to that condition.

When he came out of the bathroom, shirtless, he took his dirty clothes into the laundry room.

"We're not doing your laundry," Bill said.

"Let him leave it there," I said, and I noticed Ryan hadn't dried his back. "Your back is still wet."

Ryan finished getting dressed, and I drove the three of us to the park. I asked Ryan where he had slept, and he didn't answer. He'd nodded off in the backseat.

"Where did you sleep?" I demanded again.

He jerked awake, pointed toward the hillside, and said, "Up there." Bill and I got out of the car and scoured the hillside. We found his sleeping area on a slope between two trees, surrounded by discarded tissue from park dwellers using it as a toilet. We found his bag, minus his cell phone. Bill dropped me off at work and then took Ryan to the Resource Center.

We didn't hear anything from him for several days. Then, one night, Liz received a collect call from a "Casper" in jail on Bryant Street. Using his new moniker, Ryan said the police had picked him up for jaywalking and were holding him in jail. Apparently, there was still an outstanding warrant for his arrest from the time he'd been busted for cocaine possession in Los Angeles in 2003, and LAPD officers were coming to pick him up.

"Call Dad," Ryan told Liz. "See if he can do anything. I think it's an illegal warrant."

Ryan may be in jail, I thought, *but at least it's better than being on the street.*

That night, I told the harm reduction family group I was in that I was relieved that Ryan was at least safe. Patt, our facilitator, said, "You really think he's safe? There's no way you can keep him safe. Whether he's with you or not with you, he isn't safe. He's not safe within himself."

"Will he ever be safe?" I asked.

She shook her head. "He doesn't stand still long enough to catch up with himself. How can he be safe?"

All of my attempts to rescue him, to house him, to persuade him to go into treatment, had been my way of trying to keep him safe. The awful reality was that what I had done instead was help him stay on the run.

* * *

At that point, all the professionals in my life—my therapist, Mike; Patt, the facilitator of our harm reduction family group; and my friend Lonny—urged me to stop supporting Ryan financially. I had gradually winnowed down my financial assistance to covering his lodging, medical insurance, and psychiatrist appointments. The money with which I supported him became my last means of keeping our fractured relationship alive.

My credit card had been on file at his pharmacy to cover the co-pay for his medication, until I found out he was buying other things. I canceled the card after the pharmacist assured me that Medi-Cal (the California insurance plan for the poor and disabled) would cover Ryan's meds.

In late July, I discovered he had forged two of my checks intended for his psychiatrist. When he had told me he'd lost the checks, I had sent a replacement check directly to his doctor. I didn't discover the forgeries until I received copies of my canceled checks. Ryan had cleverly replaced the spelling of his doctor's full name with his own. Seeing the evidence of his deceit in black and white hit me harder than any previous betrayal. I felt sucker-punched in the stomach.

I wrote him a letter. "I am devastated that you have betrayed my trust. Get yourself lodging through Homeless Outreach, or get yourself into Walden House. Budget your SSDI. You're on your own."

When Liz heard what Ryan had done, she was outraged and, in some last display of daughterly protection, contacted him directly. "How could you bring yourself to steal from Mom?" she asked him.

"I didn't have any money to eat," he said.

The days after I wrote the letter were excruciating. Being out of touch, having no contact—even negative contact—with my son was, in many ways, worse than dealing with his endless crises. I began to understand my underlying codependence. Even though my attempts to get him into treatment had not been successful, they had given me something to do in an impossible situation. Each inquiry created an artificial relationship and staved off hopelessness.

When I discussed this with my therapist, he suggested that perhaps I was trying to buy a quick fix. I was horrified by the metaphor.

"You're trying to deal with the problem without really look-ing at it," Mike said. "What is your need to continually engage the problem?"

"The *problem* being my son?"

"Exactly."

"Well, I can't just walk away from him. I don't want him to die on the street."

"Yes, he's your son, but what are you ignoring when you give him money or a check he can forge and cash? The money you give him doesn't go toward food . . . he can get free food at any soup kitchen in the city. The money you give him goes toward drugs."

Until I'd discovered the forgeries, I hadn't accepted the fact that my continued financial support was feeding Ryan's drug habit. Mike continued, "You're trying to make him accountable, but he's beyond accountability. You're trying to keep him from hitting bottom, but you can't. He has to find his own way. His only chance is to stumble to his own survival."

My childhood had not trained me to walk away from chaos, to admit, "This is not mine to figure out." Growing up, I was always trying to make my alcoholic mother better, protect my sister from my mother's anger, and prevent the next crisis. Walk-ing away was never an option. If I found my mother passed out on the floor, I picked her up and got her into bed. If she was in a rage, I locked my sister in her room. I tried whatever I could to fix the situation.

Mike said, "Say no, with love. Say, 'I love you, but I can't give you any money.' Say, 'I love you, but I can't help you anymore.' Avoid being violated, and still love him."

I was reluctant to follow Mike's advice. I felt like I was still abandoning my son. Acceptance without interference proved absolutely daunting. Yet I had to borrow faith from those who had walked this path before that doing nothing with love could give my son the opportunity to find his own way.

chapter 16

the seduction of hope

At the beginning of August, a month after the forgeries, I severed my financial support of Ryan. My ninety-year-old father and his wife, Ginny, came for a visit from Florida. I arranged a family dinner at an Italian restaurant in North Beach. We allowed Ryan to use our apartment to shower and change before the meal. I even ironed a shirt for him. He had had a nonconfrontational and affectionate lunch that day with his grandfather, so I was encouraged about the upcoming evening.

However, Ryan nodded off in our car on the way to the restaurant. I wasn't too concerned at first, because he told us he had not slept the night before. When he nodded off again at the restaurant, though, I became alarmed. "Why don't you order some coffee?" I said. When it arrived, he stirred most of the contents of the sugar bowl into his macchiato with his knife. Bill looked away.

Liz arrived with her husband, Paul, and their two little girls, all dressed up in their princess finest. Everyone exchanged excited greetings, hugs, and kisses. My father, a handsome, Irish-looking man with graying hair and a barrel chest, pulled out presents he had brought for them from their recent trip to Alaska: Eskimo dolls, T-shirts, and jewelry.

We eventually ordered dinner. Ryan and my father ordered oysters, something they had always shared when Ryan worked for Dad's advertising agency in Manhattan. Over appetizers, he consumed two more macchiatos and the basket of bread. He started to slip under the table and mumbled unintelligible phrases about the vendors on the beach boardwalk in Venice. Then he got up and went outside to bum a smoke. I sighed with relief when he left the table. No one said anything about his odd behavior; we just continued eating as he came and went every five minutes or so.

After we finished the main course, Liz took her daughters to the restroom and Bill went to the men's room. At that point, Ryan was somewhere outside and had left Ginny, my father, and me at the table. Ginny, who was in her mid-eighties, a short, petite, thin-lipped, woman with a slightly severe edge, took that opportunity to address me.

"I don't know how you stand it," she said.

I thought she was being compassionate and replied, "Yes, it's been a very hard year."

But then she gathered steam, pointed her diamond-bejeweled finger at me, and said, "You're not going to like what I'm going to say, but I've got to say it. You are destroying everyone's life to save one."

"How dare you say that to me?" I said. "You're telling me I should leave my son on the street to die because you're being inconvenienced at dinner? I'm sorry you can't tolerate this, but this is what we're dealing with. I'm doing the best I can to cope with an impossible situation."

Ginny did not reply. I'm sure no one had ever spoken to her like that. I felt an urge to wring her neck. I got up from the table and went outside to calm down. The night was warm, and couples were strolling in Washington Square Park, across from the restaurant. I was still shaking when Bill came to find me. I told him what had happened.

"Well," he said, "you've got to take some responsibility for exposing your father and Ginny to Ryan."

That comment did nothing but fuel my anger. "I didn't know what shape he was going to be in. He was fine today with Dad. I can't believe you're taking Ginny's side. I need your support, not your criticism." Bill said nothing and walked away, leaving me on the sidewalk.

When I calmed down enough to go back to the table, my father moved over to sit next to me. He put his hand over mine. It was warm. I thought he was going to say something comforting. Instead, he said, "Meg, blessed are the peacemakers."

In all the years I had known him, he had never quoted the New Testament before. I removed my hand. "Don't give me this peacemaker bullshit," I said. "Talk to your wife. She should be the one making peace."

"She didn't mean what she said," he said. "It didn't come out the right way."

"Well, then she shouldn't have said it. She has no right to tell me I'm destroying everyone's life. She doesn't know what I'm dealing with."

Ryan returned to the table, and the conversation ended. After the waitress brought our desserts, a pall fell over the table.

We paid the bill and got ready to take my father and Ginny back to their hotel.

On the way to the car, Ginny took me aside. "My words did not come out the way I intended," she said. I nodded but had nothing to say. I didn't know who I was most upset with—Ginny, Ryan, or myself. We got into the car and dropped them off at their hotel. Since they were leaving early the next morning, it was time to say good-bye. I felt depressed about the way the visit had ended. My attempt to gather everyone together to have an old-fashioned family dinner had been a disaster. We took Ryan back to our apartment, and he left to sleep on the street.

It was when I opened my bathroom medicine closet that I discovered Ryan had consumed half a bottle of my sleeping pills before we'd left for dinner. He showed up the next morning to apologize for his conduct the night before. When I asked what had provoked his abuse of my meds, he justified his behavior by saying that being with Ginny and Bill made him nervous.

"That's no reason to steal my medication. How could you think that taking sleeping pills before meeting Pop and Ginny for dinner could end well?"

"I wasn't thinking. I shouldn't have come to the family dinner at all. I'd already had a good visit with Pop, and that was enough."

After I had cooled off, the stupidity of having invited Ryan to a family dinner dawned on me. I thought putting a freshly ironed shirt on him could create the illusion that everything was fine. Here was a man aching to shoot up heroin, and I was trying to get him to act polite at a dinner table.

The coincidence was not lost on me. The scene at the restaurant was not unfamiliar. As a child, I sat through many family dinners, all dressed up, where either my mother or my uncle was out of control and no adult commented or intervened. Outrageous, inebriated behavior was tolerated.

Addiction, whether to alcohol or drugs, distorts people's perceptions of their own behavior. What they think is normal or acceptable is often injurious to their loved ones. Since addiction stunts emotional growth and allows the addict to focus solely on self-gratification, addicts are prone to trampling all over other people's boundaries and emotions. Loving family members become inured to the abuse and minimize the addict's transgressions. David Carr describes his own chaotic, addiction-fueled behavior in *The Night of the Gun*: "To people who do not have the allergy, there is no clear way to explain the unmanageability that goes with addiction. A drunk or an addict picks up a shot or a dose because, same as everyone, he just wants to feel a little different. But it never stops there." It took Ginny's and Bill's reactions to make me aware that this type of conduct was not normal.

* * *

Bill made a decision that night at the restaurant; he could no longer back my irrational support of Ryan. During the three years we had lived together, he had helped me to care for my son, but he had reached his limit. "The conditions you've set for Ryan to be with the family are pointless. They mean nothing to him." I couldn't fault him—I blamed myself, since I couldn't stick to the boundaries I drew.

Bill wrote Ryan a letter stating he could not come to our apartment until he was in residential rehab and could show some consistent respect toward us and our property. He also said he would absent himself from future family dinners and celebrations where Ryan would be present. He wanted to protect himself from Ryan's disrespectful behavior. He ended the letter by saying he hoped they could someday repair their relationship and encouraged Ryan to get into Walden House.

Ryan wrote him back. "I respect your request and hope to regain your friendship in the future." He didn't apologize or say anything about pursuing rehab.

After Bill delivered the letter, I felt like I no longer had an ally. He had been a tremendous support to me, the only partner I'd had who hadn't run. Although I initially supported Bill, I was angry and hurt that I'd have to face my son's chaos alone.

Several weeks went by during which, according to Liz, Ryan was on and off the street. He was even held up at knifepoint and robbed of his new cell phone, backpack, and meds. During that time, he and I had no communication.

Then, in early September, I received a phone call from him at 7:00 A.M.

"I got my phone back, Mom. Some guy found it on a BART train and called me. Liz drove me to meet him last night in Daly City. I'd like to see you."

My stomach lurched. I was afraid he would want something from me.

"Why do you want to see me?"

"I haven't seen you in three weeks," he replied. "I have two job interviews today and I'm nervous, and tomorrow I have an appointment at Walden House for a medical intake."

"What does that mean?"

"I'll get to see a doctor."

"That's good," I said cautiously. "It sounds like things in your life are looking up."

"Yes," he said. "Can we get together?"

I hesitated but found myself drawn to the excited quality of his voice. I wanted to support any move he was making toward rehab. I arranged to meet him at a coffeehouse later in the week.

After the call, I struggled with this glimmer of hope. I wanted to believe he might actually get into the recovery program at Walden, but I didn't want to be disappointed again. I recalled the questions Martha had posed to me in the family support group: "What if you had no hope? What if you no longer hold out the expectation that things will change, that things will be different? What if you just acknowledge that this is the way things are?"

Ryan's tone struck me as altogether more hopeful. He did have a medical intake appointment with a doctor the next day at Walden House. It was merely a statement of fact, nothing more. Just information. But I watched myself catapult the facts into something else. *Maybe this time he's serious. Maybe this time he'll go in. Maybe this time they'll take him.*

Hope is a seductive mistress.

I grabbed for hope, and my mood lifted. I created scenarios of change—for him, for me, for the family. Even though I'd seen the shipwreck of his life, I secretly held on to the dream of an alternate life for him—where he climbed out of the mire of addiction, moved into an apartment, got a job, had a girlfriend—like he did throughout his twenties and early thirties—and stayed clean. But even as I dared to dream, I also saw that I had to stop my own addiction to hope.

chapter 17

the waiting game

At Ryan's intake appointment at Walden, he was told it would be at least six weeks before a bed would be available in the residential program. I was skeptical when he called and gave me that time frame. That sounded like another fabrication. Treatment was always looming right around the corner.

The intake counselor at Walden told him that during that time he could participate in the intensive outpatient program, but first he needed a full physical.

"The doctor found spider bites on my lower back and doesn't want an infection spreading throughout the program."

"Where did you get spider bites?"

"From sleeping on the street. Everyone has them. He's sending me to San Francisco General to have the spider bites drained and treated. He says the antibiotics will knock out the infection, but I have to go back to the hospital every day to have my dressings changed."

"Are the bites painful?"

He paused. "Very."

When we got together later that week, he asked if I would pay for lodging while he healed from the spider bites and waited for an available bed at Walden House. His request seemed innocent, but I was conflicted. I respected Bill's tough-love approach, and it appeared to be achieving some results. But it wasn't that clear for me. I didn't answer right away.

I called Patt, my harm reduction counselor, to ask for advice. She said there were no statistics that show that tough love works any better with addicts than harm reduction. "Harm reduction has more gray areas and involves more choices. Some of these choices are subject to disappointment and failure. You've had a lot of disappointments with Ryan, but you can't treat a dead addict." She paused. "For your peace of mind, maybe what you have to do is to keep him sheltered, off the street."

It wasn't an easy call to make. I knew he needed shelter, and I needed the peace of mind to know he was off the street. Before I'd found harm reduction, I had gone to several Al-Anon meetings, where members had advised me to walk away and let Ryan fend for himself. I couldn't do it at that time, and I couldn't do it now.

Bill and I discussed my desire to provide Ryan with lodging until he got into Walden House. "It's fine with me, as long as it isn't with us," he said. After seeing therapy clients one day, I helped Ryan find a room at the Bel Air, a single-occupancy hotel in the heart of the Tenderloin. I counted out $170 in cash to the manager each week. It took a month for Ryan's infection to heal.

* * *

Ryan started the intensive outpatient treatment program at Walden House on Halloween. I met him for breakfast a week later, and he described the difference between the cokeheads, speed freaks, and benzo-heroin heads in his group.

"The cokeheads and speed freaks drive me crazy. They ramble on and on and on. They can never seem to finish a thought, and they jump from one thing to the next. They tire me out. I bet that's how I sound when I'm manic," he said, smiling.

"A bit," I said.

"Twenty men and women in the group, mostly African American and Latino. Most are court mandated. They don't seem motivated to stop using."

"And you?" I asked.

"This morning, a crack addict from group went out and scored. He offered me some, and I said, 'No, thanks, man, I'm good.' That was a turning point. I want to get through this program."

He didn't say he wanted to stop using, but he did say he wanted to get through the program. I wasn't sure what that meant to him. His observations sounded more like those of a journalist doing research than those of someone seeking help for their own addiction. He said nothing about the treatment itself.

But his living environment had a profound effect on him. The Tenderloin was populated with addicts, prostitutes, and thieves, and specific territorial borders existed for each group. As Ryan walked around his neighborhood, he saw addicts who had lived on the street for years, panhandling or thieving. He didn't understand why they didn't avail themselves of Walden or other city resources. "I tell them, 'Come to Walden House. You don't have to live like this.'"

During November, the fact that he was engaged in the program five and a half days a week was a relief for me. I began to feel more hope that he would remain abstinent because of regular urine tests. But I became concerned as December loomed on the calendar. The holidays are rough for most people, but December was also the month of Ryan's birthday. He had spent his last birthday in jail, followed by the psych ward. Every Christmas had brought one crisis or another. I feared he would have a relapse.

I asked if he wanted a family dinner for his birthday or something more low-key. He said he'd like to have dinner with just me. He then relayed a recent conversation he'd had with Liz's oldest daughter, Rose, that had really upset him. He had gone to their house for dinner, and she'd said, "Why are you so crazy, Uncle Ryan?"

"What do you mean, Rose?"

"Why did you throw the flowerpot through the window on your birthday?"

"I threw it against the glass panel of the door because I was locked out, it was cold and raining, and I needed to get into the building. I probably would do it again if I couldn't get in. I was so cold."

When she didn't say anything else, he told her, "Please don't call me crazy anymore."

He started to cry as he recalled their conversation. I was surprised Rose's question had had such an effect on him. He said it was bad enough that the federal government labeled him crazy for his disability, but it really hurt when Rose called him that, too. He thought she must have heard comments about his mental health from Liz and her husband. Liz told him it was not just about the flowerpot; his behavior around the children had often been unpredictable.

What gave me hope about this conversation was that Rose's question had shaken Ryan. He was starting to care about what people thought of him. That seemed new. I attributed this new behavior to his being clean and in treatment.

For his birthday, we had a Mexican dinner and went to the San Francisco Modern Art Museum to see an exhibit of one of his favorite contemporary artists, Anselm Kiefer. He was relaxed, and we had a good time. To acknowledge and encourage his progress, I wrote Ryan a letter telling him how proud I was of his commitment to staying clean and continuing in the Walden program.

The next week, he relapsed and overdosed on Klonopin.

When Bill and I arrived at the Bel Air to take him to Liz's annual Christmas party, we found him slurring his words, barely intelligible. He thought Bill was a taxi driver taking him to Las Vegas. "Nope," Bill said, "we're going right back to the Bel Air."

When I later talked with my friends in the addiction field about the incident, they said, "What did you expect? That he'd go into Walden and miraculously stay clean? One relapse in seven weeks is not a big deal." Their comments chastened me.

As Christmas approached, Bill had to decide whether to allow Ryan to come to Christmas Eve dinner. It would be just the three of us because Liz and her family were having dinner with friends. Before the recent incident, Bill had not seen Ryan since he'd written his letter in August. In spite of Ryan's relapse, Bill agreed to invite Ryan to dinner.

At dinner, it made me happy to see Ryan in good shape, and I appreciated Bill's accepting him again. Two months of outpatient treatment seemed to be having a positive effect. On Christmas Day, we went to see Will Smith's movie *The Pursuit of Happyness*, about a man in San Francisco who pulls himself and his son out of homelessness and poverty. Ryan recognized some of the extras who lived near him in the Tenderloin. He had shared the food line with them at Glide Memorial Church. I cried watching the depiction of the men waiting for food, knowing my son, who was often homeless and hungry, had become one of them.

* * *

Two weeks later, on a rainy Sunday afternoon, Ryan arrived unexpectedly at the apartment. Sunday was his "free" day; he didn't have rehab. It was also my "free" day from seeing clients, and I was enjoying the sound of the rain as I wrote a lecture on psyche and myth for one of my psychology classes at Sonoma State University.

After he took off his sopping-wet jacket, we sat at the small kitchen table and had tea. Ryan opened the conversation. "I want to go into a residential treatment program outside the city."

This was a request I hadn't expected. I thought he was waiting to get into the residential program at Walden. "Why out of the city?"

"I don't think Walden residential will be any better than my outpatient group. Most of the guys there just got out of jail. They don't want treatment. They're only there because they're mandated. I want to be someplace where there's more recovery, with a *real* dual-diagnosis program."

"You told me Walden had a dual-diagnosis program."

"I haven't seen it."

I was immediately suspicious that all he really wanted was

to move out of the Tenderloin. He had been beaten up a couple of times since he'd moved in, and his backpack had been stolen repeatedly.

"Do you really want residential treatment, or do you just want out of the Tenderloin?"

"I've got to get out of the Tenderloin. Every day someone comes up to me on the street to sell me dope. It's a constant struggle to stay clean." He had told me this before, but now I heard a tone of desperation in his voice.

"Have you asked your caseworker at the Resource Center about public housing in other parts of the city?"

"Yes. Laurie says there's a seven-year wait."

I was unsure what was truly motivating his sense of urgency. Did he owe some dealer money? Had his life been threatened? The fear in his voice scared me. I hadn't heard it before.

"If you're really serious, I'll look into rehabs outside the city. In the meantime, check out public housing in other areas of the city."

This was the first time Ryan had actually *asked* for residential treatment since he had gotten mugged on the subway platform in his early thirties. His halfhearted attempts to get treatment in the past had had more to do with pressure from Liz and me. But this time he sounded more motivated, which gave me some hope. I started to research residential treatment programs both in the Bay Area and in Santa Barbara, where I had contacts in the field.

* * *

At the end of January, Ryan and I went to see Serenity Knolls, a picturesque treatment facility in Marin County. As we drove up to one of the weathered wooden buildings, we saw a group of middle-class white people laughing and smoking outside, near a fire pit. Dan, the director, a man in his mid-fifties with a worn complexion, tired eyes, and a no-nonsense air about him, invited me to be present at Ryan's intake interview. I was surprised to be included. Dan didn't ask Ryan's permission, and Ryan didn't seem to object.

"What's your story, Ryan? Why are you here?"

"I'm an addict."

"For how long?"

Ryan said, "Twenty years" and I broke into a sweat. *Twenty years? How could he have been using for twenty years?* I couldn't believe my ears.

"What do you use?"

"Heroin, cocaine, and Klonopin."

"And how old are you?"

"Thirty-nine."

The director took one look at Ryan and said, "Yup. You're almost forty. Forty is when men come into their power. It's time for you to stop."

My head started to spin, because that meant he had been using drugs before he was diagnosed bipolar. *How could I have been so ignorant of the extent of his use? How could this have been going on for so long without my knowing?* We hadn't lived together for almost twenty years, that was true, but still, how could I have been so clueless?

I must have blanched, because Dan asked me if I was all right.

"This is hard for me to hear," I said, feeling faint.

"Yes, I imagine it is." Dan got up from his desk to pour me a glass of water. "It's an illness, you know. It's not your fault. There's nothing you can do about it."

I could barely take in his words. I tried deep breathing to still my panic as Dan continued to recite how the program worked.

Their treatment philosophy was based on AA's twelve-Step approach, and they did not have a dual-diagnosis program. Ryan would have to continue to see his own psychiatrist in the city for meds because there was no psychiatrist on-site. He would have to detox off Klonopin before he entered the program, because they didn't take people on benzodiazepines.

Dan asked one of the residents to give Ryan a tour of the facility while he spoke with me.

"The place he's in—Walden House—is very tough, you know. It's like boot camp. Part of their philosophy is to tear people down. If he's ready to stop using, this place would be very nurturing for him. But I think it would take more than a month. He's been an addict for a long time."

He told me that one month's treatment at Serenity Knolls was $12,000 and they didn't take insurance. I thought that was steep and told him so. Later I discovered that the typical cost for outpatient addiction treatment in other facilities is least $10,000 a month and that residential treatment ranges between $24,000 and $35,000 a month. Since the cost is prohibitive for most people, including Ryan, a huge class divide exists in substance abuse programs. Minorities and the working poor cannot afford such treatment, and many insurance companies do not cover rehab services. Drug and alcohol abuse costs the US economy over $600 billion annually in hidden costs, such as increased health care, broken families, crime, and lost productivity.

Ryan returned from his tour of the facilities and told Dan he'd be in touch. As we drove back to the city, he was effusive about Serenity Knolls and the people he had met there. "I think I can learn from them, Mom. There're a couple of guys there older than I am who have some recovery under their belt. I want to be with people whose life experience I can relate to."

"My concern is that you just want to leave Walden because it's hard work. I haven't heard you say anything positive about the program, but I'm seeing a difference in you. You seem more aware of your effect on others."

"I like my counselor, Marvin. He's a black dude with a lot of recovery, but he's leaving soon—the counselors are *always* leaving to go to other programs. I need more experienced counselors to give me some wisdom."

I noticed the excitement in Ryan's voice, which led me to believe that he was serious, and I appreciated his desire to be with folks who had more recovery. But I was still suspicious of his incentive to go into residential treatment, and I found Serenity Knolls cushy and expensive. There were many reasons why I thought it was the wrong program for Ryan: it lacked a dual diagnosis component, which is what he said he wanted, there was no psychiatrist on-site, and it was beyond my budget. But I agreed to check out their success rate and research affordable programs.

chapter 18

almost forty

Six weeks after we visited Serenity Knolls, Ryan flew to Santa Barbara for a clinical interview with Safe Haven Psychiatric Center, a small, twelve-bed, dual-diagnosis treatment facility that focused on addiction and mental disorders. I had looked into several other programs in the Bay Area, but they were as financially prohibitive as Serenity Knolls, while Safe Haven was affordable and had come highly recommended by a friend in the addiction field.

I was nervous Ryan would find a way to sabotage this next step. Sure enough, while skateboarding four days before his scheduled flight, he lost his wallet and all of his identification.

"How are you going to get on the plane?" I asked, annoyed.

"Oh, that's no problem. I'll get a temporary license from the Department of Motor Vehicles."

"In two days? You know the DMV doesn't operate that fast."

"I've gotten IDs from them before. I can get it if I can borrow some money."

There was no such thing as "borrowing" money where Ryan was concerned. He never paid back money he "borrowed" from anyone. What he really meant was, *Will you* give *me the money for the ID?* Instead of arguing with him about paying me back, I gave him the cash because I wanted him to get on that plane. United Airlines confirmed he could use the temporary identification card, along with his Social Security card.

Bill took Ryan to the airport and stayed with him until he got through security. We were both afraid that at any point there would be a mishap. Ryan was thinner than usual at this point, and, in spite of fairly warm weather in February, he was wearing a dark, heavy winter coat with a furry hood pulled up around his head. When Bill saw a security guard pull him out of the line and pat him down, he worried they wouldn't let him through. But after the pat-down, Ryan turned around to smile and wave at Bill and walked to his gate.

Upon his return, he was excited. He rambled on and on, barely taking a breath, as he paced back and forth in the kitchen about how well his interview had gone.

"I met with Cindy, the clinical director, and told her I'm really serious about my recovery."

"Did she ask you how long you've been using?"

"Yes, I told her my addiction history. But I think they'll still take me. However, to be accepted in the program, I'll have to detox from Klonopin. But that shouldn't be too hard."

That confused me. I thought it would be hard to withdraw from Klonopin. But I didn't get to ask anything about the detox, because he was on to the next thing.

"I'm a little nervous, however, about the new, experimental anti-opiate drug they want to give me. It's called Vivitrol. It's given as a monthly injection. I haven't read about it yet, but it's supposed to eliminate the craving for opiates like heroin. I guess it's like Antabuse for alcohol."

Cindy told him he would probably be in treatment for six months, with the possibility of supervised aftercare. "That seems like a long time, don't you think? I can probably do it faster. I don't want to be there for six months. I still want to study to become a paralegal."

"If they think it'll take six months, they probably know what they're talking about. You're dealing with a twenty-year addiction. And their brochure states they have vocational training."

Ryan got quiet. Then he said, "The last thing she mentioned was that she only wanted clients who would contribute to the harmony of the house. It's a small house. I hope I can find a friend."

This forward movement was new for Ryan. It was encouraging that he was talking about a future. Still, I had my fears. He revealed that Walden House had recently put him on methadone because of his Klonopin abuse. I chose not to question him, but I knew methadone was used as a substitute for opiate use, and although Klonopin can be addictive, it is not an opiate; it's a benzodiazepine. A week later, he admitted that his slip with Klonopin was actually for morphine sulfate, an opiate readily available on the street and ingested by heroin addicts. My intuition had been correct. He was still manipulating the truth.

* * *

As Ryan started to get better, I told my harm reduction family group that I was becoming more anxious and my insomnia had increased.

173

Patt asked, "Why do you feel more anxious now? He's been doing well for the last four months."

"Yes, I know. But I don't believe I can trust it. I've been disappointed too many times before. Frankly, I lack faith."

"Maybe it's also because you're picking up that if he doesn't get into residential treatment soon, there's going to be a crisis."

I knew she was right. Ryan had instigated this whole search for treatment outside the city because he was scared of continuing to live in the Tenderloin. I figured he was afraid of someone in particular. He probably owed someone money, and drug dealers don't tolerate druggies who don't pay their debts. I felt thunderclouds gathering, and I didn't know how to prevent the storm. At the same time, I knew I could do nothing to prevent a crisis except wait. Either the crisis would materialize or he would be accepted at Safe Haven. But I was not good at waiting. Not only was I not sleeping, I felt like I was always holding my breath.

Ryan received a call the following week to confirm his acceptance, but there was no bed currently available. For the next six weeks, Safe Haven kept postponing the date of his admission, based on the delayed discharge of another client, who had relapsed and needed more treatment. At first it was the end of February, then the end of March, and finally the end of the first week of April. During that time Ryan continued at Walden, had bimonthly appointments with his psychiatrist, and continued to live at the Bel Air. But the uncertainty of the timing of his admission was nerve-racking for us all. I talked Jerry into contributing to the cost of Safe Haven, but he was wary of treatment programs because of their poor success record.

Although I was relieved that Safe Haven had finally committed to a date in early April, the timing could not have been worse for me. Months before, Liz, her daughters, Bill, and I had made plans to fly to Florida to visit my father and Ginny over the Easter weekend. Liz had found very inexpensive, nonrefundable airline tickets. If I chose to drive Ryan to Safe Haven, instead of flying to Florida, not only would I disappoint my father, but Liz had said, "Don't you *dare* think of canceling."

As the date drew closer, my angst over this decision grew. Ryan's behavior did not help. Without his favorite counselor, Marvin, at Walden House, he lost his resolve. He began to show increasing signs of anxiety about the change he was soon to make. His speech got rapid and pressured, he didn't keep appointments, and then he went missing for a couple of days. In a panic, Bill and I called every hospital in the city, as well as the county jail, but he was nowhere to be found. When he did finally answer his cell phone, it was clear he was high. My fear that he would sabotage his admission to Safe Haven unless I personally escorted him there intensified.

We finally settled on a workable plan. Liz's husband, Paul, who was not going with us to Florida, would take Ryan to the airport for his flight to Los Angeles. There, Jerry would meet him and drive him to Santa Barbara. Bill found a flight that left San Francisco early enough in the morning to accommodate the time of his intake appointment at Safe Haven. To make it foolproof, Paul arranged to have Ryan stay with him overnight to get him to the airport. This arrangement did not alleviate my worry, but I flew to Florida as scheduled.

Once there, I could think of nothing else the day of Ryan's departure. I was completely obsessed with whether or not he had gotten on the plane. I was no fun at the beach with my granddaughters, I couldn't concentrate on conversations with my father, and Liz finally said, "You might as well have stayed home; you're certainly not here with us."

Finally, I called Paul at work to find out if Ryan had departed as planned. The news was shattering. Ryan hadn't stayed with Paul the night before and had not been at the Bel Air when Paul had gone to pick him up at 5:00 A.M. Paul drove around the deserted streets of the Tenderloin and finally found him on a street corner, completely loaded. He rushed him back to the hotel, helped him pack, and sped to the airport. Not surprisingly, Ryan missed his flight.

It got worse.

Paul then helped Ryan arrange a ticket for the next scheduled flight. But Ryan didn't make that flight either, and for the rest of the day no one knew where he was. Jerry kept calling the airline and eventually found out that airport security had taken him to the nearest hospital because he was mumbling incoherently. When he was released, still partially incoherent, he was put on a flight. Jerry picked him up in Los Angeles, put him up in a motel, and drove him to Safe Haven three days later. But during that time, I didn't know whether he was dead or alive.

My reaction to the stress of the whole escapade was to total my father's car. After the community Easter-egg hunt was over, I put his car in reverse and the gas pedal stuck. Sliding across the slick, wet grass parking area at thirty miles per hour, I took out two cars parked behind me. When I was able to pull my foot off the pedal and jam on the brake, I slid even farther. I jumped out of the car, shaking with spent adrenaline, relieved I had not run over a small child holding an Easter basket filled with colored eggs and chocolate bunnies. But I had totaled a brand-new black

BMW, which, the owners angrily pointed out, still had its dealer tags on it.

The police were generous that day. They let me go. Liz said with disgust, "Well, Ryan ruined our Easter holiday without even being here."

My father's insurance paid for the three cars, and my insurance paid for my whiplash and yearlong visits to the chiropractor. Safe Haven admitted Ryan, despite his urine's testing positive for cocaine, Klonopin, and heroin.

It was a bleak beginning.

chapter 19

can we help him or not?

Living in a house with eleven other residents was a tough adjustment for Ryan. He was used to complete freedom, to coming and going at all hours of the day and night. At Safe Haven, he had to share a bedroom, follow a schedule, attend groups or classes all day Monday through Saturday, and do chores, and his movement was restricted to the house. The program was structured on a step basis with four levels to move through, each of which allowed more freedom and privileges. Ultimately, at level four, the residential clients were able to leave the house to volunteer doing jobs in the community.

Ryan was resistant to the program from the start. In our first phone conversation after week one, he had a litany of reasons to leave.

"I don't want to stay here. The program is much too basic. This isn't an addiction treatment facility; there are no other addicts here beside me."

"Basic? What are you talking about, 'too basic'?" I choked back a scream. "You're in there for treatment, not to evaluate the program."

"They only have one group devoted to addiction that's a dual-diagnosis group and one AA meeting a week once you get to level three."

"So what? You wanted a dual-diagnosis group, and now you've got one. Do the work to get to level three so you can go to an outside AA meeting. Don't make excuses about there not being enough addicts in the program. Why would you want to be surrounded by addicts?"

Unfortunately, this sounded similar to his complaints about Walden House: the program was too basic and didn't treat the types of addicts he wanted to associate with. His focus was always on the negative, instead of on how he could use the program for himself.

He went on to complain about the other residents of the house. "None of the residents here have ever held a job. That's not me," he said. "They have serious mental illnesses and are on heavy-duty meds. And *that's* not me. I want to get on with my life."

It was clear that he didn't want to see himself in them. He refused to acknowledge that he had a serious mental illness, and, even worse, I colluded with him by not refuting his denial. I don't know what prevented me from saying something at the time; maybe it was because he hadn't asked for this illness and I always felt guilty that he suffered with it. Or maybe I just couldn't admit to myself that he had a serious mental illness, and persuaded myself that being bipolar wasn't that bad. By not confronting him with the obvious evidence of his own mental illness, perhaps I could absolve myself of my own sense of guilt.

I changed the subject, avoiding the obvious, and asked him about his cognitive therapy group. It was supposed to help him address his negativity and modify his impulsive behavior. He found fault with that, too.

"It's very theoretical, I'm not learning much. Look, I just can't justify the expense of being here. Seven thousand dollars a month is a lot of money. I should have researched Safe Haven more closely. It's definitely not an addiction program. I want to go back to Walden."

I couldn't believe it. How could he not see that he was just like the other residents? His life was unmanageable: he was in residential treatment, he was addicted to illegal narcotics, and he didn't have a job or anyplace to live. It was clear he had no ability to reflect on his own situation. I asked him if he had found anything positive about the program.

"Yes, I'm learning to cook. Last night I helped Chris cook a pork roast for the house."

"That's good; cooking's a skill you can use when you get out."

"But these aren't my people."

I felt completely thwarted; no matter what I did to try to help him, he would find a way to reject it. I thought this program would give him a chance to learn some tools to deal with his mood swings, develop social and work skills, get on his feet and get a job. But, listening to him, I realized he didn't want to do anything to help himself. I lost patience with his excuses.

"If you don't stay at Safe Haven and get the most you can out of the treatment, I'm not going to spend another penny on you. I'm not supporting your return to San Francisco and Walden House. I hope you understand that. You'll have no place to go unless you stay there and graduate from level four."

As I listened to my voice, I wondered if I could trust my words and back them up with action. My threats had been empty so many times before. And Ryan counted on that.

During the following two weeks, Ryan seemed to settle down and moved from level one to level three. Dr. Katz, the psychiatrist at the facility, took him completely off Klonopin. Ryan said he was experiencing some anxiety but didn't want to take a substitute medication to treat it. He was afraid of the side effects of other anti-anxiety drugs. His ultimate goal, whether prudent or not, was to eventually taper off all psychiatric medications. I was completely opposed to that idea, having witnessed his manic episodes when he went off his medication.

The second week he was there, he was given his first injection of Vivitrol, the anti-opiate drug, which caused him some mild stomach problems and insomnia. The vocational director told him he would soon be able to do part-time volunteer work at Santa Barbara Legal Aid and that there was the possibility of taking paralegal courses in the area.

It was Safe Haven's policy to involve the residents' families, but Ryan had to sign a release to give staff permission to talk to us. I was asked to check in with Ryan's caseworker, Marguerite, for an update on his progress each Tuesday morning—even while I was on vacation in Florence, Italy. This was before cell phones, so I stood in the foyer of my small hotel, trying to hear her above the din of construction workers arguing behind me. When Bill and I had arrived the night before, the hotel manager had failed to inform us that the hotel was being remodeled and there was no phone service in the rooms.

In the first couple of phone calls, Marguerite had commented about how likable Ryan was, how intelligent, how creative, and what a great sense of humor he had. She was upbeat and positive, and that had alleviated my apprehension. But this time she paused and cleared her throat. "I have to let you know I'm feeling a bit cautious because Ryan doesn't seem to realize what a grip his addiction has on him. I question the strength of his motivation."

I shook my head silently. *Oh, no—here it comes*, I thought.

"Can we help him or not?" she continued rhetorically. "That's the question. He doesn't seem to have much insight about how his comments and behavior affect other residents. It's hard to help someone who lacks self-awareness."

I was taken aback by her comment. Didn't she know that lack of insight was a symptom of bipolar disorder, part of the illness Safe Haven said they were equipped to treat?

"How much insight do you expect him to have?" I asked. "He's been there only three weeks."

I wondered why she was questioning whether they could help him at Safe Haven. They had presented themselves as a facility with a high rate of success among residents who stayed in treatment for six months.

"Are you giving up on him already?" I asked.

"Oh, no, I'm just concerned about his lack of self-awareness. A person can't change if he can't reflect on his behavior." *That's true*, I thought.

Marguerite's comments conveyed a subtle warning. When I later repeated this exchange to Myrtle, one of my colleagues at Sonoma State, she said, "Sounds to me like they're getting ready to get rid of him." I had willfully ignored that possibility, but I feared she was right.

During Ryan's fourth week at Safe Haven, Marguerite called

with concerns that he was trying to get himself kicked out. He had been disrespectful to staff and made fun of some of the residents with serious illnesses. He also made vulgar remarks about women and gays.

"The group called him on his offhand comments, but he didn't seem to understand he was inappropriate. He's been demoted to level one until he can change his attitude."

I was shocked by Ryan's alleged juvenile, prejudicial slurs. This was a side of him I didn't know, and it disgusted me. Part of me, however, started to make excuses for him in my heart. Maybe he was just irritable as a result of his withdrawal from Klonopin and street drugs. Maybe Safe Haven didn't have the experience they said they had working with heroin addicts. But Marguerite disabused me of that notion. "We're used to dealing with all kinds of drug abusers, but we won't tolerate disrespectful behavior from anyone. He'll remain at level one until he improves his interpersonal skills."

I knew he was going to be angry at being dropped to level one, but Marguerite was adamant. "We also need the support of both his parents," she said. Ryan had tried to lobby Jerry to help him leave during the first week of his treatment, but I knew Jerry was willing to give Safe Haven a chance.

"You have my full support, and I think you have Jerry's, too," I said. "I also hope Safe Haven has tools beyond punishment to address behavioral change. I thought you used a form of cognitive therapy to deal with poor impulse control."

"We do. But Ryan doesn't respond to cognitive therapy. He doesn't like it."

Ryan was indeed distressed by the demotion; he had expected to start working at Legal Aid but now couldn't do so.

He tried to justify his vulgar language by saying he had been joking. "I'm used to much tougher language in the Tenderloin."

"Well, you're not in the Tenderloin, so clean up your act," I said.

He didn't take any responsibility for hurting anyone with his comments but agreed to treat everyone with respect and keep his mouth shut.

I didn't believe him. I knew he was capable of sabotaging the program if he wanted to, so I reminded him that my financial support would end if he got himself kicked out.

"You've been given a gift to help you turn your life around. Don't throw it away."

* * *

The following week, Ryan was still "frozen" at level one. He was outraged that his demotion would lengthen the duration of his stay. "It's a ploy by Safe Haven to make more money," he argued. Marguerite told me the staff felt threatened and intimidated by his anger. She reminded him that if he behaved at a job the way he was acting at Safe Haven, he would be fired. "I'd never act that way at work," he said.

Cindy, the clinical director, told him she would not tolerate his disrespect of staff and residents and his undermining of the program. A family meeting was scheduled for the following Thursday to determine whether Safe Haven would allow Ryan to stay. I drove down from San Francisco, and Jerry drove up from Los Angeles for the meeting. I had not seen Ryan in six weeks; he had gained weight and looked healthier than he had in years.

He was happy to see us, and I was happy to see him, too. But I was not prepared for what came next.

We met in Cindy's office, along with Marguerite, Ryan's case-worker; Todd, the dual-diagnosis coordinator; and Walker, the director of vocational services. Cindy was a tailored, dark-haired woman in her early forties. For a moment, I was impressed with her stylish, pointy-toed, high-heeled shoes. However, the atmosphere of congeniality immediately turned frosty as she took charge of the meeting and addressed Ryan.

"You have a decision to make during this meeting. Either you're in this program or you're out—you decide, yes or no—but unless you change your attitude, you're not staying here. You have sexually harassed one of the women clients by calling her a 'fucking cunt.' I will not let you harm other residents. I'll give you a three-day discharge notice for interpersonal issues if you don't turn your behavior around *now*."

I was taken aback by her fierceness, as well as by the language she said Ryan had used on one of the women residents. He tried to explain himself, saying he had not said what he was accused of, but she rebutted him, stating that several staff members had overheard him and had e-mailed her about what had transpired. She then read quotes from the e-mails, and Ryan said nothing to deny them. I was deeply shaken by the hostile sexual remarks Ryan was accused of making. What Marguerite had told me on the phone was true.

Ryan tried to change the subject by bringing up his concerns about the side effects of Vivitrol. He had just had his second injection of the anti-opiate drug and had experienced more side effects, including chest pains. Because of his damaged heart valve, he was concerned about continuing with the injections if there was a possibility of negative cardiac results. He wanted to see the research about the drug.

Cindy turned to me. "I gave you the literature before he started the program."

"No, you didn't." The only thing she had sent me was an advertising circular from the pharmaceutical company about its use for alcohol dependence. It didn't describe side effects for those coming off opiate use. She got up, went behind her desk, and rifled through papers, looking for the information. She turned to Ryan.

"If you're not going to take the next Vivitrol shot, then we can end this meeting right now. That was a condition of your admittance."

Jerry leaned forward and tried to support Ryan's concern about Vivitrol. "He certainly has a right to read the literature," he said.

Cindy cut him off abruptly. "You're being hostile, and I will not tolerate that here." Jerry sat back in his chair. He had raised his voice slightly to be heard, but he had hardly been hostile. Without missing a beat, she returned her attention to Ryan.

"You're endangering the other residents with your attitude about authority. You think you're smarter than everyone else here, and you think you can get away with whatever you feel like. I will not let you take the other residents down. I am a shark, and I am going to circle around you. I will know what you are doing every moment of the day."

Her tirade shocked me. I understood her obligation to protect the other residents, but her hostility toward Ryan, Jerry, and me seemed excessive. In fact, she was projecting her own hostility onto Jerry. I'd never heard anyone describe herself as a shark before. She obviously didn't like Ryan and had made no bones about it. She handed him the literature on Vivitrol, told him to go over it, and ended her participation by telling him he had until ten o'clock the next morning to decide whether he was going to continue with Vivitrol. If he didn't make a commitment to changing his behavior, he was out.

"If you have any questions," she said to Jerry and me, "you can ask Marguerite, Todd, or Walker." She got up, excused herself, and left for another meeting. It was only after she left that I realized I wasn't breathing. As I looked around, it seemed as if no one else was, either.

* * *

I asked Todd, the head of the dual-diagnosis program, if he thought Ryan was bipolar. He said he hadn't had enough direct contact with Ryan to know, because he didn't have him in a group. "But I've heard good things about you from some of the other group leaders," he told Ryan.

"I'm glad to hear something positive," Ryan said.

"Apparently, you know the twelve steps so well you could teach them, but it doesn't sound like you're integrating the principles into your own life. From what Cindy's saying, you don't walk the talk outside of group. We'd all like to see you do better."

Jerry asked Walker to explain how Ryan's demotion to level one affected the vocational program. He addressed Ryan directly, reassuring him he could still intern at Santa Barbara Legal Aid once he moved back to level three. "And I found a paralegal program for you to attend here in Santa Barbara once you get to level four."

Marguerite told Ryan she had heard good things about his participation in the art and poetry groups. He smiled. It was clear that even though Todd, Walker, and Marguerite had positive things to say, they were there to support Cindy's position and to let him know he was on notice. Marguerite summed up Cindy's conditions.

"I hope you make the decision to stay here, because the program has a lot to offer you. I'll do my best to support you if you decide to cooperate, but you have to show more motivation to change."

Ryan nodded. He had been fairly quiet during the meeting, sustaining eye contact with whoever addressed him and looking at me from time to time to gauge my reaction. I had started to cry at one point during Cindy's litany of offenses. I didn't know whether his calm exterior meant he had, in some way, shielded himself from Cindy's accusations and hostility or if he had tuned her out. She had interrupted him every time he tried to defend himself. I certainly wasn't able to tune her out, however; my legs were weak as I walked out of the meeting.

* * *

While I was getting together with some former teaching colleagues, Ryan had dinner that night with Jerry to discuss the Vivitrol issue and his behavior. The next morning, Ryan told Cindy he would continue with Vivitrol for two more months and turn his behavior around. Regardless of Ryan's renewed commitment, by noon Cindy had decided Ryan was not sincere. A staff member reported that Ryan had reiterated the vulgar, objectionable phrase, and when he tried to explain he had merely been repeating to one of the residents what he'd been accused of saying, he was told it was too late.

Cindy left a message on my cell phone stating she was discharging Ryan for interpersonal issues. She said I could call Marguerite for a discharge plan and Ryan had seventy-two hours to get out. Cindy didn't return my repeated phone calls. I called Marguerite to find out why he was being kicked out. She said Ryan was overheard making derogatory comments about Cindy, including calling her a "shark."

"She called *herself* a shark in the meeting," I said. "You heard her."

"Yes, but Ryan also said he was going to *get* her," Marguerite said.

"Meaning what?"

"I don't know, but we don't tolerate threats."

The decision could not be reversed; they had already given Ryan many chances. When I asked what the discharge plan was, she said, "Ryan should be in a treatment program." That infuriated me.

"I know that. That's why we invested in Safe Haven to begin with. What's your plan for him now?"

"There is no plan. You can either pick him up or leave him on the street."

I couldn't believe my ears. "Leave him on the street? Where do you expect him to go?"

"He'll have to figure that out."

When I went to pick him up two days later, a young staff member told me that if Ryan left that day, a Sunday, he would be leaving AMA (against medical advice). When I pointed out that there was no discharge plan and that he had been told to leave the premises within seventy-two hours, she said that was all she knew. I was baffled and frustrated. Cindy never returned my calls, and Ben, the director of Safe Haven, was "unavailable."

Ryan and I went out to breakfast to discuss what to do. I had to drive back to San Francisco that day for work the next morning. Ryan wanted to have one last conversation with Ben to ask if they would reconsider their decision to discharge him, or at least to give him a refund (which they refused). He would remain overnight at Safe Haven to do so. We'd get a train ticket for Ryan to San Francisco as a failsafe before I had to leave.

He started to talk about the positive aspects of his stay at Safe Haven. He had been clean and sober for six weeks and had stopped using Klonopin. He had decreased his use of trazodone, which he had been prescribed for sleep. Living with residents who had more serious mental disorders than his made him wonder if he was truly bipolar. "Maybe my problem all along has been substance abuse."

"I don't know," I said. "It's too soon to tell." While he was reflecting on his experience, all I could think about was one of David Carr's observations: "To be an addict is to be something of a cognitive acrobat. You spread versions of yourself around, giving each person the truth he or she needs—you need, actually—to keep them at a remove." Ryan was trying to put a good face on having been thrown out of treatment—treatment that he himself had asked for—and I was heartbroken that another attempt at getting him help had ended badly.

chapter 20

the *pietà* redux

I was more than heartbroken; my spirit was crushed. I had naively thought that Safe Haven was going to be the magic bullet—that Ryan would detox from Klonopin, respond positively to the treatment, learn to manage his cravings for opiates, and start on a path to self-sufficiency. Like many well-intentioned family members, I believed that if I got Ryan properly treated and appropriately situated, the addiction would go away. My fairy-tale image of Ryan's recovery was completely unrealistic. Now I was left to wonder whether Ryan had purposely sabotaged his treatment or whether the sabotage had been an aspect of his mental illness. Perhaps Safe Haven had been a poor choice. And, of course, it was possible that Ryan was just not ready to deal with his addiction. I was reminded of what Oliver Sachs wrote in *On the Move*: "We are destined, whether we wish it or not, to a life of particularity and self-development, to make our own individual paths through life."

I called Safe Haven's psychiatrist, Dr. Katz, to see if he had some answers. I had spoken to him once before, and, unlike the other professionals at Safe Haven, he was accessible. When he returned my call, I asked if he thought Ryan was bipolar.

"It's too hard to tell. He was clean for only six weeks. A person needs to be clean for a much longer period of time, perhaps a year or two, to discern whether there's a mental illness or not, but he did have a tendency to mood swings and he was irritable."

"Is the irritability a symptom of bipolar disorder, or could it be related to the decrease in Klonopin?"

"It could be either. But it was more than that. He was endangering the treatment of the other clients by being nasty to some people who have been here for a long time. He made fun of a man who is deaf and harassed one of the women. He wasn't motivated to change his behavior."

At that point, everyone had told me he wasn't motivated to change his behavior. I asked Dr. Katz if all the other residents were motivated to change their behavior. Patt had forewarned me that sometimes addiction programs say "the patient wasn't motivated enough" to excuse their lack of treatment success.

Katz said that some people come into treatment at first with a defensive, inflated attitude, like Ryan, but adjust their behavior when they're knocked down a level. "Ryan wasn't willing to change his behavior," said Katz, "and he didn't have a good start, coming in with all the drugs in his system. We never saw that he was motivated to stop using. He had the words but not the actions."

I felt completely defeated. However, Katz assured me that it was still possible for Ryan to stop using. He reiterated what Dan had said at Serenity Knolls about Ryan's being on the cusp of forty. The dope-scoring lifestyle gets too hard the older a person gets. "Some people have to hit bottom first, and he hasn't yet hit bottom," said Katz. "He could turn things around if he doesn't die first."

His last statement chilled me to the bone. I thanked Dr. Katz for his time and hung up.

I don't know quite why I was so obsessed with knowing whether Ryan was bipolar. Part of me didn't want to accept that he was disabled with a mental illness, and another part didn't want to accept that he was an addict. I wanted to understand how these illnesses interacted with each other. Did the mental illness leave him vulnerable to addiction, and did the addiction amplify the symptoms of his bipolar illness? If I could just figure it out, get to the bottom of it, maybe the therapist in me could help him get better. I was still hopeful that his bipolar medication could manage his mood swings and erratic behavior. But if he was caught in the grip of his addiction, as Marguerite had said he was, there was nothing I could do.

* * *

Later that month, I revisited the *Pietà* at the Saints Peter and Paul Church. I needed to spend time with Mary to learn about grace during overwhelming sadness. I was struck, as I had been before, by the way she cradled the body of her dead son on her lap, holding him with her right hand, her left hand open to the heavens in a gesture of surrender. She had witnessed her son's life journey, but she could not prevent his suffering and death. She was powerless over his destiny; she had done all she could do.

In trying to get Ryan into treatment at Safe Haven, I learned

I couldn't control whether he was accepted or not and, more importantly, I couldn't control whether he stayed there and accepted what they had to offer him. He clearly demonstrated that his life was not mine to control. I was powerless over his choices. I could only make decisions that concerned my own life.

* * *

Three weeks after he returned from Safe Haven, Ryan visited our apartment. He arrived sporting a heavy, dark beard and wearing a woman's snug white leather coat. He looked like a city nomad who walked the streets day or night. Over a cup of tea, I told him I was heartbroken about his discharge from Safe Haven.

"I'm having a really hard time accepting that you got yourself kicked out, Ryan."

He looked at me intently. "Look at me, Mom. I'm off Klonopin, and I've been clean for nine weeks. Just because I didn't stay at Safe Haven doesn't mean I'm not moving forward in my recovery. Recovery's a bumpy road."

"I realize that; it's bumpy for me, too," I said.

He held my gaze as he continued. "Recovery's more than abstinence; it involves clear, sober thinking. And I've been thinking a lot more clearly since I left Santa Barbara. I've found a room out of the Tenderloin, I'm trying to get back into Walden House, and I'm looking for a job. It might seem like one step forward and two steps back, but I feel good about the decisions I've made."

I was not convinced by his words, but I congratulated him on his abstinence. I had been so invested in a certain rosy outcome that it was hard for me to see the progress he said he was making. When he left, I told him I loved him but asked him not to call me for a week. I needed a break from his chaos.

He called the next day. He needed a copy of his identification, which he had just lost. My request was meaningless.

* * *

I had allowed Ryan's addiction and the chaos that came with it run my life for the past three years and, to a lesser degree, for the past eighteen. When he went into Safe Haven that April, I wrote him a letter outlining the conditions of my financial support and telling him I was weary of the crises that accompanied his addiction. "I want my life back," I wrote. "I want to get on with my life." I realized that what I was doing was asking Ryan to give me *my* life back by working *his* recovery. I wanted him to get help so I would feel better.

What I needed instead was to fully embrace my inability to change Ryan and to take charge of my own recovery. I no longer wanted my life, feelings, and desires to be contingent upon his choices. I had to figure out what I was *willing* to do—which included walking away for a time-out or paying for his lodging. At that moment, I didn't know what I would do, but I certainly had to let go of my fantasies about Ryan's recovery.

I hated to admit it, but my over-involvement in his life had gotten in the way of his recovery. My years of paying for his rent, medical insurance, psychiatric treatment, and urgent visits to the hospital had done nothing to make him responsible. I have compassion now for how enmeshed I was with my son, but my inability to accept the reality of his illness perpetuated the dynamics of our relationship.

Of course, when I knew he was sleeping on the street, a part of me was there beside him in the gutter. But I didn't have to linger there. I needed to move on and get back to my life. I wanted to be present for those loved ones who deserved a full me, not a divided me. I had a loving and compassionate man in my life, a wonderful daughter, and beautiful granddaughters, and I wanted to enjoy being part of their lives.

By 2007, I had decided to go back to graduate school to pursue a doctorate in psychology, something I had started but had not finished twenty-five years before. Bill and I moved from San Francisco to Santa Barbara, both for my studies and for my work. When I told Ryan's psychiatrist I was moving, he said, "I think it's a good idea. You never know how much your desire to help can turn into enabling."

* * *

While Ryan was at Safe Haven, I imagined ending this book on a hopeful note. I wanted to demonstrate how love, patience, and compassion could conquer all. Instead, I had to come to terms with the limits of a mother's love. The reality is that Ryan's life got temporarily better, then progressively worse.

Four years after Safe Haven ousted him, Ryan found his bottom in a judge's four-year prison sentence for having received a stolen laptop and having been present at a burglary. I wasn't prepared for him to fall that far. The judge's words continue to echo in my mind.

"You come from a good background, you've had a good education, you've suffered no hardship: four years."

* * *

For the next three years, I drove from southern California to the Bay Area every other month to visit Ryan at San Quentin. He was clean and sober, and, despite eating prison food, he looked healthier than I had seen him in decades. He received medication for his bipolar illness daily. When I commented on how clearheaded he seemed, he agreed. "The structure in my life creates a sense of stability." His mind, body, and brain were all getting a much-needed cleansing and respite.

He had a prison job as a clerk for correctional officers, and he attended a writing class once a week with the Zimmerman brothers, twins from Berkeley who volunteered their time to work with prison inmates. He took a printmaking class, along with "lifers" who worked together to make linoleum prints, and he created a mural of a Diego Rivera painting in the building he shared with two hundred inmates. It was designated an "honor dorm" because the inmates housed there were low-level offenders who either had jobs within the prison or took classes.

The highlight of every day for Ryan was the 4:00 P.M. mail call. He'd write to friends and family alike, desperate to stay in touch, to remind them of his existence, and to hear word of the "outside." He called me collect once a week when he could access one of the four phones designated for all the men. He decided to write stories about his life, so we discussed character development, structure, and how to make believable the chaotic episodes he had experienced.

I told him that I was writing a book in order to come to terms with how mental illness and addiction had affected our lives—his, Liz's, Bill's, his dad's, and, in particular, mine.

"I'm not happy about this," Ryan said. "I don't want my whole identity to be wrapped up with mental illness and addiction. I'm afraid you're going to write about only the negative things and leave out all the positive things about our relationship."

"I can understand that," I said. "But I'm not writing this to please you. I'm writing about my own experience, not yours. I'm trying to understand my own cycle of denial and rescue attempts and ultimate powerlessness to prevent you from ending up here. It's for my own healing, and also for the countless mothers and fathers in the same position as me who are trying to do the best for their child in an impossible situation."

"I don't want you to use my name."

"I'm not. And I hope that at some point you might like to add your own perspective to the book."

"We'll see."

chapter 21

reflections from san quentin

Ryan did decide to add his perspective to the book, specifically his insights about his bipolar illness. After a year of incarceration, he dictated his thoughts to me over a series of twelve-minute collect calls from prison. Week after week I took notes, transcribed them, and read them back to him the next time he called. It was a collaborative process. It was also the most sustained and insightful conversation we had ever had about his illness.

"One reason I struggle with my diagnosis of manic depression is that it presents an implicit compromise of autonomy, of an independent sense of self. It is hard to swallow the idea that something simultaneously mysterious and empirically definable has such power over my ego, over a comprehensive sense of my identity and purpose.

"I experience a type of existential suffering when I'm in the grips of a serious depression. The terrible paradox is that even

though there is redemption of mood and hastening toward pro-
ductivity on the other side, it is still difficult to soldier on. The
defeat is crushing, and the weight of it all is burdensome to the
people around me. Those who are my constant, most vigilant
support, like my mother, are the ones who most acutely suffer
with me. It might be a different kind of experience than dealing
with a loved one's physical ailment, but it must be just as infuri-
ating and hopeless.

"We give more weight to physical ailments, such as cancer,
AIDS, Lou Gehrig's disease, Parkinson's, or leukemia, that are
scientifically quantitative, and less to mental illnesses that are
not as easily definable or treatable. Individuals who don't have a
mood disorder think that if only a person with manic depression
would make a concerted, disciplined effort, they could change
their mood. Even though psychiatrists, neurologists, and physicians have pointed to the mechanisms of faulty brain receptors,
in our oversimplification, we still think, as does the collective,
that a mood disorder can be licked. We just need to make the
necessary change, whether it is to our work, relationships, reli-
gion, belief systems, or environment.

"Depression is the price paid for mania. Depression is earth-
bound. It is a muddy, slow morass, being oppressed by an unre-
lenting blanket of heavy gray fog. Mania, on the other hand, is
quick, clear, full of muse, fire, and creative energy, all with a nod
toward the heavens. At their best, manic episodes are full of pro-
ductivity, craving, pleasure, desire, and connection. To be envel-
oped and protected by mania is to be in a euphoric, comfortable
place. It sounds like a wonderful high, and the tendency is to
want to live in that state, but it can also lead to dissociation and
sometimes delusions, fantasy, and paranoia.

"I have lived with manic depression long enough to understand the pitfalls, crises, and tragedies brought on by mania and its attendant rationalization. The view from inside is never as drastic as the view from outside, however. The fantasy inherent in mania and exacerbated by drugs, either prescribed or illicit, pits me against the other: the psychiatrist, the loved one, the family member. While chaos surrounds me, I delude myself into thinking I have control, or, worse, that something good will come from the insanity. While in the grip of mania, I find it more difficult to see the consequences of my actions. I have viewed my mania as a rationalization for my addiction. This is the selfish nature of a mood disorder inextricably linked with addiction. Manic behavior is the ultimate expression of self-involvement.

"There is a difference between the self I know and the self that other people see. I try to accept myself as a unique, creative personality, rather than being defined by the disorder. This uniqueness of personality is complicated by the need to escape this personality; I don't understand this. Perhaps it is as simple as being exhausted and wanting normalcy. Perhaps it is the need to escape marginalization."

* * *

My journey is the untold reality of countless mothers and fathers who try to "fix" their sons or daughters and fail. We are all defeated in the face of mental illness and addiction. Because my son was gifted and bright and continued to function at a high academic level in high school and the first year of college, I missed the early signs of his illness. After he was diagnosed in his early twenties, I believed his job losses, broken relationships, and failed friendships had to do with the mood swings related to bipolar illness. I had witnessed his manic phases, and I knew there were times when it was difficult for people to be around him. I was sad but not surprised when girlfriends left him, disappointed but not unsympathetic when bosses fired him. I thought if he just got on the right medication and found a talented psychiatrist, he'd become stabilized and his life would go back to "normal." Over the last two decades, I've learned there is no such thing as "normal." It's just a six-letter word.

It took me years to accept that the losses in Ryan's life were also related to something even more difficult to manage than mental illness: drug abuse. I was stunned to find out that close to 80 percent of individuals with bipolar disorder are plagued with a substance abuse problem. For a long time, I conspired with my son's denial about his drug use, wanting to believe he was telling me the truth. I didn't realize how deeply ingrained family denial about generational addiction ran in my veins. I come from a long line of functional Irish American alcoholics. I refused to accept that I enabled his addiction by supporting him financially when he lost jobs, and that I did not hold him accountable to agreements we had made. Denial was easier than facing the truth. Being hooked on hope protected my heart from despair.

When I did acknowledge Ryan's drug abuse, I was frantic to save him, terrified he would die without my help. I was compelled to rescue him before he hit bottom. I offered him the best treatment I could find and afford. My efforts to rescue were ultimately unsuccessful. Hope propelled me forward but also kept me blind. My focus on Ryan also hurt my daughter. Although I could not accept it at the time, Ginny's statement to me about hurting others to save one was accurate.

I found that the pattern of isolation that addicts and those suffering from mental illness experienced also holds true for family members. I was overwhelmed as a single mother, and that hampered my ability to step back and see clearly. I am aware that my focus on Ryan's bipolar illness, my denial about his drug use, and my ineffective rescue attempts over many years prevented him from taking responsibility for his own illness. It wasn't until I listened to the stories of other family members in NAMI, harm reduction family groups, and Al-Anon that I began to understand the complexity of mental illness and drug abuse. They helped me to examine how my own addiction to rescuing him interfered with accepting my son's illness.

I still struggle to find compassion for my powerlessness in the face of his challenges.

chapter 22

dawn

At dawn, my fourteen-year-old granddaughter, Rose, Bill, and I sat on the cold wooden bench outside the gate at San Quentin. The night before, Rose had asked to go with us to prison to be there for her uncle Ryan's release.

"Are you sure you want to get up at 5:00 A.M. to drive out from San Francisco to San Quentin with us?" I asked. "It's going to be cold and dark. And there's no guarantee he'll get out."

"Yes," she answered. "I might want to write a short story about it, and I'll never have an opportunity like this again."

"Let's hope not," I said, smiling.

The gate opened, and a white van passed through it and came to a stop. I tried to look in the window of the van, but it was blacked out. I quickly gave my iPhone to Rose to videotape Ryan's release.

"Just don't let the guard see you," I said. She nodded.

A heavyset female guard climbed out of the driver's seat and came around the front of the van to slide open the side door.

Ryan stumbled out, wearing a white T-shirt and jeans, holding a cardboard box of his belongings.

With a big smile, Ryan came over to where Rose, Bill, and I were waiting. He put his box down on the bench, looked me in the eye, and gave me a big hug.

"How's the book coming?" he asked.

"It's finished."

resources

This is not a complete list but may be helpful in a crisis.

WHAT TO DO IN A MENTAL HEALTH CRISIS:
The following suggestions about what to do in a mental health crisis are adapted from Mental Health First Aid USA. They also have informative webinars on their website: http://www.mental healthfirstaid.org/cs/first_aid_strategies.

Mental Health First Aid teaches a five-step action plan, **ALGEE**, to provide help to someone who may be in crisis.

Assess for risk of suicide or harm
Listen non-judgmentally
Give reassurance and information
Encourage appropriate professional help
Encourage self-help and other support strategies

Assess for Risk of Suicide or Harm: When helping a person going through a mental health crisis, it is important to look for signs of suicidal thoughts and behaviors and/or non-suicidal self-injury. Some Warning Signs of Suicide include:

- Threatening to hurt or kill oneself
- Seeking access to means to hurt or kill oneself
- Talking or writing about death, dying or suicide
- Feeling hopeless
- Acting recklessly or engaging in risky activities
- Increased use of alcohol or drugs
- Withdrawing from family, friends, or society
- Appearing agitated or angry
- Having a dramatic change in mood

If you don't know whether or not your loved one is exhibiting warning signs of suicide, always seek emergency medical help. If you have reason to believe your loved one may be actively suicidal, call the National Suicide Prevention Lifeline: 1-800-273-TALK (8255).

Listen Non-judgmentally: It may seem simple, but the ability to listen and have a meaningful conversation with an individual requires skill and patience. It is important to make an individual feel respected, accepted, and understood. Mental Health First Aid teaches individuals to use a set of verbal and nonverbal skills to engage in appropriate conversation – such as open body posture, comfortable eye contact and other listening strategies. I tried to listen non-judgmentally but when Ryan started to talk about drugs I got increasingly scared. Even though I am trained as a psychotherapist to listen non-judgmentally, I'm sure I radiated my fear and panic.

Give Reassurance and Information: It is important for individuals to recognize that mental illnesses are real, treatable illnesses from which people can and do recover. When having a conversation with someone whom you believe may be experiencing symptoms of a mental illness, it is important to approach the conversation with respect and dignity for that individual and to not blame the individual for his or her symptoms.

Encourage Appropriate Professional Help: There are a variety of mental health and substance use professionals who can offer help when someone is in crisis or may be experiencing the signs of symptoms of a mental illness.

Types of Professionals
- Doctors (primary care physicians or psychiatrists): have your doctor's number handy or call your local hospital emergency room and ask them what to do
- Social workers, counselors, and other mental health professionals
- Certified peer specialists
- Types of professional help: "Talk" therapies, trauma therapy
- Medication: expect that in a mental health emergency, your loved one will probably be put on medication to stabilize them
- Other professional supports

Encourage Self-Help and Other Support Strategies: There are many ways individuals who may be experiencing symptoms of a mental illness can contribute to their own recovery and wellness. These strategies may include:

- Exercise: It was clear that when Ryan rode his bike 30 miles up the Pacific Coast Highway, he was trying to regulate his stress level so that he could fall asleep.
- Relaxation and Meditation
- Participating in peer support groups: Today there are chat rooms on-line to give support to people experiencing a mental health crisis.
- Engaging with family, friends, faith, and other social networks. It is important for your loved one to feel safe and supported by loved ones.

WEBSITES FOR MORE INFORMATION AND REFERRALS:

NAMI (National Alliance on Mental Illness): http://www.nami.org offers an array of support and education programs for peers, families, college students, and Vets that help build better lives for the millions of Americans affected by mental illness. I took the Family-to-Family program, which I found invaluable in helping me understand my son's illness. Find your local chapter by contacting the Information HelpLine, which is an informational and referral service. Call 1-800-950-NAMI (6264) or email at info@nami.org

The American Foundation for Suicide Prevention (AFSP): http://www.afsp.org is exclusively dedicated to understanding and preventing suicide through research and education, and to reaching out to people with mood disorders and those impacted by suicide.

The Center for Mental Health Services (CMHS): http://www.sambsa.gov/about chhs.aspx is the Federal agency within the U.S. Substance Abuse and Mental Health Services Administration (SAMHSA) that leads national efforts to improve prevention and mental health treatment services for all Americans.

Child and Adolescent Mental Health: http://minh.nih.gov/health/topics/child-and-adolescent-mental-health/index.shtml is a section of the National Institute of Mental Health's website which provides a great deal of information on the mental health issues and concerns of childhood and adolescence.

Children's Mental Health Network: http://cmhnetwork.org is a weekly update of what's going on in state and federal research in mental health for children and adolescents.

Healthy Minds.org: http://www.healthyminds.org http://www.healthyminds.org/ is the American Psychiatric Association's online resource for anyone seeking mental health information. Here you will find information on many common mental health concerns, including warning signs of mental disorders, treatment options and preventative measures.

Al-Anon: http://www.al-anon.org

Alateen: http://www.al-anon.alateen.org/english.html

Alcoholics Anonymous: http://wwwlalcoholics-anonymous.org

Narcotics Anonymous: http://na.org

Partnership for a Drug-Free America: http://www.drugfree.org

Hazelden: http://www.hazelden.org

National Association for Children of Alcoholics (NACoA): http://www.nacoa.org

The Center for Harm Reduction Therapy (HRT): http://harm reductiontherapy.org

selected readings

Amador, Xavier. *I Am Not Sick, I Don't Need Help! How to Help Someone with Mental Illness Accept Treatment*. New York: Vida Press, 2010.

Carr, David. *The Night of the Gun*. New York: Simon & Schuster, 2008.

Conyers, Beverly. *Addict in the Family: Stories of Loss, Hope, and Recovery*. Center City, MN: Hazelden, 2003.

Denning, Patt, Little, Jeannie and Adina Glickman. *Over the Influence: The Harm Reduction Guide for Managing Drugs and Alcohol*. New York: The Guilford Press, 2004.

Fontaine, Claire and Mia Fontaine. *Comeback: A Mother and Daughter's Journey Through Hell and Back*. New York: Regan Books, 2006.

Greenberg, Michael. *Hurry Down Sunshine: A Father's Story of Love and Madness*. New York: Other Press, 2009.

Jamison, Kay Redfield. *An Unquiet Mind: A Memoir of Moods and Madness*. New York: Alfred A. Knopf, Inc. 1995.

Kennedy, Patrick J. and Stephen Fried. *A Common Struggle: A Personal Journey through the Past and Future of Mental Illness and Addiction*. New York: Blue Rider Press, 2015.

Knapp, Caroline. *Drinking: A Love Story*. New York: Dial Press, 1996.

Miklowitz, David J. *The Bipolar Survival Guide: What You and Your Family Need to Know*, 2nd Edition. New York: The Guilford Press, 2011.

Moyers, William C., and Katherine Ketcham. *Broken: My Story of Addiction and Redemption*. New York: Viking, 2006.

Myerson, Julie. *The Lost Child: A Mother's Story*. New York: Bloomsbury, 2009.

Shavelson, Lonny. *Hooked: Five Addicts Challenge Our Misguided Drug Rehab System*. New York: The New Press, 2001.

Sheff, David. *Clean: Overcoming Addiction and Ending American's Greatest Tragedy*. New York: Houghton Mifflin Harcourt, 2013.

Sheff, David. *Beautiful Boy: A Father's Journey Through His Son's Addiction*. New York: Houghton Mifflin Company, 2008.

acknowledgments

The author would like to acknowledge the teachers of the Family-to-Family courses sponsored by NAMI (National Alliance for Mental Illness); the members in my Monday Al-Anon group; Patt Denning, director of the Center for Harm Reduction Therapy in San Francisco; photojournalist and friend, Lonny Shavelson; therapist and wise mentor, Mike Denney; addiction specialist C. D. Taylor; my dear friends, Susan King and Kim Bancroft for their probing questions and close editing; my colleagues at IWWG, particularly Eunice Scarfe, Susan Tiberghien, Pat Carr, and Myra Shapiro who have consistently supported my writing; my Thursday morning memoir group for their insights, feedback, and humor; and my family, particularly, Bill for his love and patience as I struggled to give birth to this book.

about the author

Meg McGuire is a mother, writer, psychotherapist and the author of five internationally published nonfiction books. She is an activist in mental health and criminal justice reform and teaches memoir writing in southern California.

selected titles from she writes press

She Writes Press is an independent publishing company founded to serve women writers everywhere. Visit us at www.shewritespress.com.

All the Ghosts Dance Free: A Memoir by Terry Cameron Baldwin. $16.95, 978-1-63152-822-4. A poetic memoir that explores the legacy of alcoholism and teen suicide in one woman's life—and her efforts to create an authentic existence in the face of that legacy.

Insatiable: A Memoir of Love Addiction by Shary Hauer. $16.95, 978-1-63152-982-5. An intimate and illuminating account of corporate executive—and secret love addict—Shary Hauer's migration from destructive to healthy love.

A Different Kind of Same: A Memoir by Kelley Clink. $16.95, 978-1-63152-999-3. Several years before Kelley Clink's brother hanged himself, she attempted suicide by overdose. In the aftermath of his death, she traces the evolution of both their illnesses, and wonders: If he couldn't make it, what hope is there for her?

Fire Season: A Memoir by Hollye Dexter. $16.95, 978-1-63152-974-0. After she loses everything in a fire, Hollye Dexter's life spirals downward and she begins to unravel—but when she finds herself at the brink of losing her husband, she is forced to dig within herself for the strength to keep her family together.

Warrior Mother: A Memoir of Fierce Love, Unbearable Loss, and Rituals that Heal by Sheila K. Collins, PhD. $16.95, 978-1-938314-46-9. The story of the lengths one mother goes to when two of her three adult children are diagnosed with potentially terminal diseases.

Three Minus One: Parents' Stories of Love & Loss edited by Sean Hanish and Brooke Warner. $17.95, 978-1-938314-80-3. A collection of stories and artwork by parents who have suffered child loss that offers insight into this unique and devastating experience.